CALL ME A COUNTRYPOLITAN

CALL ME A COUNTRYPOLITAN

RICK EDDINS

Published by Advantage, Charleston, South Carolina.
Member of Advantage Media Group.

Printed in the United States of America.

ISBN: 978-1-59932-088-5
LCCN: 2008937774

Dedication

To Sherry, my wife, with thanks for all that has been and all that will be.

Acknowledgements

I have wanted to write a book about my life for a long time. I collected newspaper articles, wrote notes to myself, thought up outlines and even began to write several times. But I could never really get started. It became apparent to me that even though I have the gift of gab, I don't have a gift for writing. My problem was solved when Dr. Bob O'Keef, my former pastor, agreed to help with the project. Bob and I would meet each morning for about two hours. I would spin my tales and he would take notes. He would then put the stories I had told that day into written form. *Call Me A Countrypolitan* would not have become a reality without Bob's gift of writing. His gift of writing and my gift of gab were a spectacular union. I don't know how many hours we spent together over the months of talking and writing, but each hour was a joy and the result was this book.

Countrypolitan would also never have been a reality without the support of my wife, Sherry, and our children, Jennifer and Kevin. The three of them are so much more to me than family. They have supported me in all of my life's adventures. They have loved me, encouraged me, strengthened me and guided me. Sherry, as my soul mate and best friend, has made me so much more than I could ever have been on my own.

I owe more than my life to my parents, Herbert and Flonnie Eddins. The values I live by and the virtues I try to follow came from them. Most parents try to teach their children all of the things they need to know to succeed in life. My parents did more than teach – they showed me by their daily lives.

When I married Sherry, I was fortunate to join a fantastic family. My father-in-law, Audree Long, had a very successful career with Piedmont Aviation. Sharing his business experiences with me has been invaluable. His corporate world view is so different from my small business experience that he has always challenged me to think outside the box. I thank him for putting up with a son-in-law who has often needed his good advice.

I thank those who have read, edited, and proofed the manuscript for *Call Me A Countrypolitan.* It is an incredibly important part of putting a book together which often goes unnoticed. But I noticed.

And I thank all of the people in my life who have made the stories in *Call Me A Countrypolitan* so real. Since all the stories are true, the people in them are truly fascinating. I thank God that they are.

Foreword

"Call Me a Countrypolitan" is a collection of stories. These are stories of life, of love, of politics, of faith, of business, and more. Put together, it is the "not quite finished" saga of my life. I share these stories because each of them has taught me something important.

Life is a continuing lesson. Our failures and our successes are tutors, desperately trying to teach us something. Our everyday experiences mold our character, determine our values and give direction to our future. Or they should!

There are times in all our lives when we are too busy to listen, too convinced that we know enough to learn anything new and too stubborn to hear the voices that could change our lives. But once in a while a voice breaks through or life forces us to listen.

These are stories of the voices that I have heard that have molded me: the voices of my grandmothers, my father, my wife; the voices of preachers and politicians, of murderers and victims of crime, of irate citizens and grateful constituents. There is even the "still small voice" of God.

I hope that as you read these stories, you will be reminded of the voices that have molded your life. I also hope that you will be encouraged to listen more carefully to the voices around you. We are all guilty of not listening or of listening to the wrong voices. We need to learn, again, how to turn off the 'noise' of life and listen to the voices that really matter. Together, we might all learn something.

Contents

Chapter 1

Call Me a Countrypolitan

"The country is lyric, the city dramatic. When mingled, they make the most perfect musical drama."

—LONGFELLOW

Pigs don't know pigs stink. Ultra liberals don't know just how stupid some of their ideas really are. Ultra conservatives don't know just how heartless some of their ways are, just as cosmopolitans don't know that some country folk are really sophisticated. In fact, most of them think that country people are all bumpkins.

Call me a countrypolitan. I know that the word "countrypolitan" doesn't exist, but I'm going to coin it. It describes me perfectly. It's a blending of country boy and cosmopolitan.

I was raised in the rural section of Wake County, North Carolina. Wake County is the seat of North Carolina government. Raleigh, the capital city, is located in Wake County and is one of the fastest growing cities in the United States. Urban sprawl is overtaking the county and the entire region. Wake County and the surrounding areas are going the way of Tidewater, Virginia, Northern New Jersey, and Southern California. We are fast becoming a metropolis.

If the current growth continues, within the next twenty years or so, there will be a great crescent city of urbanization stretching from Greenville, Rocky Mount through Raleigh, Durham, Chapel Hill and continuing through Burlington, Greensboro, and High Point to Lexington, Salisbury and Concord to Charlotte and Gastonia – one great city, a golden crescent with many different names. A raging economic boom and massive immigration from the "Rust Belt" states have, and will continue, to make central North Carolina a businessman's paradise.

I live in North Raleigh. And, I love it. I love all of the advantages of a great city – the social, educational, artistic, business, and sports opportunities are phenomenal. Raleigh rivals any great American city.

But it hasn't always been that way. I was raised in a far different place. When I was born in 1953, Raleigh was one of the smallest state capitols in America. It was a sleepy, southern town. When the interstate highway system was first laid out, Raleigh was the only state capitol in the nation which was not scheduled to have an interstate. It seemed to be too insignificant a town to warrant such a road.

Wake County was mostly rural. Dotted with small towns and smaller crossroads communities, Wake County was a farming center. Though the state government was the largest single employer in the area, farming dominated the economy. The small towns (Wake Forest, Knightdale, Holly Springs, Garner, Zebulon, Apex, and Cary) were really small, and the crossroads communities (Rolesville, Fuquay-Varina, Willow Springs, Morrisville, Wakefield, and Lizard Lick) were even smaller. I was reared in the country near Rolesville. We had a Knightdale phone number and a Wake Forest address, but I attended school in Rolesville.

We would go to Wake Forest to do the grocery shopping and to pay most of the bills. It was a sophisticated little town. In fact, before the big city of Winston-Salem stole it, Wake Forest University was actually in Wake Forest. (Southeastern Theological Baptist Seminary is now housed in the former university buildings.) The town was opulent, without being showy.

Rolesville was the place that we went to hang out. Rolesville was little more than a crossroads. Until the 1970's there were no stoplights, and from the 70's through around 2000 there was only one – at the only real intersection in town. The intersection was town-center. Located at each of the four corners were a couple of stores. There were two grocery stores, side-by-side in the same building. There was a livery stable for mules; a mom and pop drugstore, and a country store. There was a gas station and town hall. Two churches, Rolesville Baptist and Rolesville Methodist, were slightly removed from the intersection, about a city block away. About 200 people lived in the greater Rolesville area.

It was in Rolesville that I became acquainted with, grew to love, and was proud to be associated with "country people." There was a small country store near my home (just a country mile away) where the men of the community would gather after supper (during the summer months) or in the afternoons (during the winter when farming chores were less) to talk, play checkers or dominos, and generally hang out. The men had a bond of friendship that was punctuated with laughter. Country people love to laugh. If catching a black snake and putting it into the cab of your neighbor's pickup truck would bring everybody a laugh, then it was worth the effort. Laughing together was important because country people lived a hard life.

All the men talked about "coming through." As a boy, I wasn't always sure what they meant by that, but as I listened to the men gathered around the kerosene space heater in the store, I learned. Many of the men had grandparents who had fought in the Civil War, all of them had fathers who had served in World War One, and nearly all of them had served in World War Two. They had "come through."

And, all of them had "come through" the Depression. The Depression hit every section of the country hard – Wake County was no exception. Country people had the means of getting through it better than city folk. They could grow their own food, can the vegetables, dry and mill their corn for flour, grow enough cotton to spin thread for clothing, and generally make it without much money. There were some farmers however, that didn't "come through." Crop prices fell so dramatically that many farmers couldn't raise enough money to pay their mortgages and they lost everything. Those farmers who did make it through had a tremendous appreciation for life, and they were determined to live life to its fullest.

Country people are faithful people. Churches dotted the landscape. The church I attended was called Wake Crossroads Baptist. There was a steep staircase rising from the road to the front door – the stairway to heaven. Country people know that faith isn't easy. Sometimes faith is a hard and steep climb. There were so many faithful people at Wake Crossroads. There was the Deacon Board – the men who sat up front, nearest the pulpit. They were the "saints" who had the long string of perfect attendance pins hung from their jackets. Everyone wore their Sunday best. If Jesus were to come, you didn't want to be caught wearing something less than your best. If Jesus were to come during the week, He would expect you to be wearing work clothes, but not on Sunday.

My parents were not regular church goers, but they saw to it that I was "sent" to church. I'm glad they did. I was introduced to the kind of people who know the value of hospitality, true Christian hospitality. They had a warmth about them that penetrated me to the depth of my soul; I suppose it was the love of God, or the grace of Christ, or the power of the Holy Spirit. Whatever it was, it was a joy to climb those steep steps on Sunday mornings. It was kind of like going home.

Two-year old Rick, dressed for a trip to Wake Crossroads Baptist Church, stands on the steps of Mammy's house.

Country people knew how to "take time" with you. They often took time around a meal of some kind. Whether it was the men at the store who would decide to have a fish fry with bass and bream caught from the neighborhood pond, or the women of the church providing a feast in covered dishes, or one of the local farmers barbequing a pig and inviting the whole town. There was always a feast of some kind and though the food was always great, it was not just the food, which nourished me. It was the time that was spent talking and just hanging out that filled me. Every Saturday night, one of the local country stores would push everything back, bring in as many wooden chairs and benches as the place would hold, cover the benches with feed sacks to make them more comfortable, and invite the community to hear the local guitar and banjo pickers play and sing country music or gospel. Folks would sit around, nursing a "co-cola" – only Yankees called it "Coke," and we had never heard the terms "pop" or "soda" – eating Moon Pies or Nabs, and just taking time with each other. The music was pretty good, too.

Rick's first Christmas Feast, 1953.

Country people aren't perfect. They have an independent streak that sometimes results in downright lawlessness. There was a local county constable who sold moonshine from an old abandoned tobacco barn at the back of his property. He reasoned that the county didn't pay him enough as a constable to make a living, and many of the men in the community were glad to help out by buying some of his shine. It was their Christian duty. There was a problem, however. About eighty percent of the people were Baptists, and Baptists don't drink alcohol – at least, not openly. I'm told that the constable would make appointments with some people who came to buy so that the deacons wouldn't risk running into each other out by the barn.

The people of Rolesville taught me to be a country boy; to cherish hard work, community, laughter, faith, self-sufficiency, and creativity. They taught me to take the time to live life to its fullest. They taught me that people who are too heavenly minded are of no earthly use, and that people who are only earthly minded are no good either.

I know that there are "country" people everywhere. There are some who live in big cities, even some who live up North. But if they live in any of those places, they have some kind of rural background, some kind of connection with farming and the soil, some kind of tie with growing things. Country people have learned, even if they never plant a seed, to grow good people.

Sometimes it's hard for a country boy to live in the big city. But when a country boy takes the time to look around, he can find that the sophistication of the city has some real advantages. The Raleigh, Durham, Chapel Hill area is home to three of the greatest universities in the world – listed here in no particular order – N.C. State, Duke, and UNC. There are other colleges, universities, technical colleges, community colleges and trade schools of all kinds. These colleges have spectacular libraries, incredible theater programs, fantastic musical productions, and powerful athletic teams.

The Triangle of cities is host to one of the world's foremost research areas. Called the Research Triangle Park, the facilities located within its bounds are some of the premier high tech industries and businesses in the world, employing literally thousands of professional people. The economic impact is measured in the billions of dollars annually.

Raleigh has one of the best public school systems in the country. And Raleigh is home to beautiful neighborhoods. Raleigh has a "we can conquer the world" attitude. Raleigh is as racially diverse as any city in the South, and people of all colors and national origins get along great! There are art and history museums, an opera house, a concert hall that is home to the North Carolina Symphony, and Memorial Auditorium which hosts traveling Broadway productions that are every bit as good as Broadway.

Quite simply, Raleigh is a wonderful place. And Raleigh, with all of its sophistication is full of country boys (and girls) who have fit right in. It is a city, which has embraced its rural, Southern, small-town heritage while celebrating a new vision to be a world-class city.

Raleigh is a great place to be a countrypolitan or a cosmopolitan. I fit right in, either way.

Chapter 2

Outhouses and Outdoors

"People will not look forward to the future with hope who never look backward to their ancestry."
—EDMUND BURKE

Claudia Young was my Mom's Mom. But the only name I ever knew her by was Mammy. Visiting Mammy was always an experience. The extended stays in the summers were the highlights of my childhood.

Mammy lived on the family farm between Louisburg and Bunn. Her house was a typical southern farmhouse. It was a two-story, wood clad dwelling with a four-column porch on the front and a lean-to porch on the back. Having two porches was essential in the South – you could move to where the breeze was and the sun wasn't.

Mammy's farm was a sheer delight for a little boy. There were just so many things to explore:

- The family cemetery where most of the graves were marked with simple stones on which no names were inscribed.
- All the barns. Country people never threw anything away and each barn was a treasure trove.
- The coal pile near the giant willow tree. Each lump of coal was a potential diamond. If Mammy would just fix me a cape with a big "S" on it, I'd be Superman.

- The still "active" outhouse. It wasn't so much a place to explore as to use. I have never understood why wasps like outhouses. So using it may not have been an exploration, but it sure was an adventure.

My cousin, Juan, and I were fast friends. We played together, fought together, swam in the creek together, and explored the fields and the woods together. We took great pleasure in finding crawdads (that's crayfish to any Yankees who are reading) along the ditches, which bordered the fields. We spent hours in the mornings enticing doodlebugs out of their holes and hours in the early evenings catching fireflies.

Mammy looked great; her house needed a little TLC, but she was happy with it just the way it was.

Visiting Mammy was best done in early summer. If I visited her in the late spring I got caught up in all of the work of planting. And if I was there in mid to late summer, it was harvest time. It was in the lazy, hazy days of early summer that Juan and I could play to our hearts' content.

And there were plenty of things to play with. We didn't have store bought toys. We didn't need them. Tobacco sticks were great toys. A tobacco stick was a hardwood stick that was about an inch square and about three and a half feet long. Tobacco leaves would be tied to them and they would then be hung in the barns to cure.

When tobacco sticks weren't being used for real work, they were great playthings. They made great swords to fight the pirates who were trying to steal the farm. Held to the shoulder, a tobacco stick was a sharpshooter's rifle, perfect for repelling those invading blue boys from the North. Held to the side, and accompanied by a rat-a-tat-tat sound, they were sub-machine guns for killing off the Nazis and the Japanese.

Mom strikes a pose by tobacco sticks.

It's amazing what a kid's imagination can do. Parents today need to turn off the computer games, confiscate the cell phones and iPods, throw away the TV remote controls, and lock the kids out of the house. They'll grumble and gripe for a little while. They'll complain, "There's nothing to do." But don't let them back in the house. After a couple of hours of complaining, their creativity and imagination will kick in. And they might just turn out to be kids.

Echoes

Tobacco sticks aren't just good for war games. They're also great for trying to roll barrel hoops. Keeping a hoop rolling down a dirt road takes tremendous skill. It requires hand-eye coordination, perfect timing, and the ability to run as far and as fast as the hoop rolls. It's a great game to play alone. It's even better when two people and two hoops are competing for the same space.

It was on one of these adventures of hoop rolling that I met Robert walking down the road. He was carrying a rusted, worn out plow point. Wearing bib overalls and clodhopper shoes he looked every bit the part of a country bumpkin. But there was something different about Robert.

Not only was he as old as the hills, or so it seemed to a young kid, but he was also blind. You could tell by one look in his eyes, but you couldn't tell by any other way. He didn't have a cane. He wasn't being led by anyone. He simply knew where he was.

Blind Robert made his living by walking the back roads of Franklin County and collecting scrap metal, mostly used plow points, from all of the farmers. Everyone knew him and everyone was glad to support his business.

Blind Robert knew where he was because he knew the sounds of Franklin County. He knew the particular sound that each creek made and the particular squeak of each gate. He knew the slam of a door with a good spring and the thud of a door whose spring had sprung.

If Blind Robert ever got to a place that he wasn't quite sure of, he would stomp his foot on the hard-packed dirt road (or clap his hands if it had been raining) and listen for the echo. He knew the distinctive echo of each house, each barn, and maybe even each tree.

Blind Robert taught me something important. He taught me that we need to listen to the echoes. Too often in our lives we fail to hear the echoes of our words. We fail to hear the echo of our insensitive comments, so often spoken without thought. What damage have they done? We don't hear the echo because we don't want to listen to our hate-filled words.

In double jeopardy, we have also failed to hear the echoes which would do us good. We have not really listened when people have thanked us for good work. We haven't heard, really heard, the cry of the needy. We've been too busy to listen when our children cry out for discipline, or our spouse's desire for tenderness.

Maybe we're too busy rolling hoops, or catching doodlebugs, or playing war, or going to work.

Blind Robert taught me a lesson that day. Listen. I wish that I remembered it more often.

Community

It was when I visited my other grandmother, MaMa in mid-summer that I was first introduced to real work. It was tobacco-harvesting time. In those days, it took an army to harvest a field of tobacco.

PaPa takes a break from priming in his tobacco fields.

The primers were the people with the toughest job. Priming tobacco consists of harvesting the bottom leaves, which have ripened. Tobacco leaves usually grow in threes around the stalk and a good primer could reach his hand around the stalk and break off all three leaves at once. He would put the leaves under his other arm and move on to the next plant. The primers never stood up straight because it would break their rhythm. Hour after hour, day after day, of leaning over was truly "back-breaking" work. The primers would continue priming all the way down the row until they reached the sled

A mule almost always pulled the sled. Being the mule driver was a pretty good job, because you got to stand up straight all day, but standing at the south end of a northbound mule is not always pleasant. Mule drivers were responsible for keeping the mule happy enough that it would do its job. There is nothing more stubborn than an unhappy mule. And there are no people in the world who are unhappier than a crowd of primers with a row-full of tobacco under their arms and no place to put it.

When the sleds were full, they would be dragged to the tying barns. Another army of people would take the tobacco off the sleds and hand it to those who would tie it to the sticks. The tied tobacco would then be hung in the barns, which required another group effort.

It was in the tobacco fields that I was introduced to gospel singing. As the primers primed, or the handers handed, or the tiers tied, they sang. In five, or six, or even seven part harmony I would hear the words of faith:

"Rock of Ages cleft for me. Let me hide myself in thee."

"When the role is called up yonder, I'll be there!"

"Amazing Grace! How sweet the sound that saved a wretch like me!"

When I was priming, I prayed that a rock would open up and hide me. When the sun bore down on my aching back, I knew that I would be hearing the roll-call most any minute. And then, I would indeed be saved.

From way off, I could hear it. It wasn't the sound of the heavenly choir, but it was just as wonderful. It was the sound of MaMa's dinner bell. Oh that clank was sweet.

From the fields and the barns people gathered around the makeshift tables MaMa had set up in the yard. And on the tables was every kind of good country rib-sticking food that you could imagine. From fatback to fried chicken, from butter beans to navy beans, from cornbread to biscuits, it was all there. MaMa had spent the whole morning cooking. It's amazing how fast an army of people can eat a feast.

It was in those fields, and around those tables, and in the top of the tobacco barns, and on the porches after lunch that I discovered true community. People with a common task working together to accomplish a common goal become a community. And people who work together, sing together. And people who eat together, laugh together.

People who laugh together and sing together and eat together learn to love each other. And more singing breaks out. It is the song of the soul. It's every bit as sweet a song as MaMa's clanging bell.

Chapter 3

Thanks, Dad!

"Follow my advice, my son; always treasure my commands. Guard my teaching as your most precious possession."
—PROVERB 7:1(NEW LIVING TRANSLATION)

Everyone has a father. Some people are blessed to have a dad. I am grateful that I had both – in one man.

Herbert Eddins was born to parents who were tenant farmers in rural Wake County, North Carolina. His parents never owned a home. As tenant farmers, they lived in housing provided by the owner of the farm, which they tended. Tenant farmers farmed for a share of the profits. It was nearly impossible for tenant farmers to make enough money to break out of the system.

There was never any security in tenant farming. There were no regular paychecks. Everything was so dependent on the weather. An unusually dry spring meant the crops would not even break the surface of the ground. Too much summer rain would rot the crops in the field. A strong windstorm in the fall would knock the ripened crops down, making it nearly impossible to harvest anything.

MaMa and PaPa dressed in their Sunday-go-to-meeting clothes.

My father was determined to break out of the system. He never graduated from high school (though later in life he received his G.E.D.), but growing up on a tenant farm had taught him the value of hard work. Somehow, he was able to convince Burlington Mills that he would be a good employee. He was hired as a cloth inspector then became the supply room clerk for the textile giant's factory outside of Wake Forest. He spent the next forty years as the best supply room clerk that he could be.

He loved to work. He was one of those people who actually enjoyed overtime. In fact, a forty or sixty hour workweek was just not enough for him. As long as I can remember, my dad had extra jobs. He always needed something more to do, somewhere else to go, some new task to complete, and some new business to build. At various times through the years he owned and operated numerous small businesses: a cleaning service, a carpet cleaning business, a barrel recycling business, a country store, and two hamburger and hot dog grills. One of his grills was in Lizard Lick, North Carolina. (You can't get more country than that.) In his fifties, he went to school to learn the art of auctioneering, and it was as an auctioneer that he stumbled into an occupation that changed both our lives – owning and operating a flea market. It really is true that one man's junk is another man's treasure.

As a father, he taught me, instructed me, and disciplined me. As a dad he showed me, guided me, led me, and loved me.

Plum Bushes

My father always said he "didn't take any crap from any kid." He was glad to correct any children, whether they were his or not, but he took great pride in correcting me. To say that he was strict would be an understatement. He was glad to enforce his strictness. He had learned the lesson that to spare the rod would spoil the child, and he was determined not to have a spoiled son.

His favorite "weapon" was a switch from one of the plum bushes outside our house. Plum limbs have little knobs all along the length of them. When I needed some "instruction," he would send me outside to pick a switch from the plum bush. I learned, the hard way, that if I picked a switch that was too flimsy, or didn't have enough knobs on it, my "instruction" would be more intense. (Thinking back, I wish that Roundup had been around. I would have sprayed every plum bush on the place).

As I recall, the switching was very effective. I can't remember how many times I had to get a switch, but I do remember that every time was well deserved. As an adult, I have been described in many ways, but I have never been called "spoiled." Maybe we should all plant plums in our yards.

A Stick-built House and a Hand-dug Well

Since my father was raised in a tenant house, he was determined to have his own place. He had been working at Burlington Mills for several years and paying $35 a month in rent. He didn't make enough money to get a traditional mortgage from a bank. He couldn't afford to buy a house that was already built or to pay someone to build him a house. But he had a friend who was willing to loan him $5,000 on "just a handshake."

With the money, he purchased an acre of land and the materials to build a house. He set to work. The house was small – two bedrooms, one bath, a kitchen, a living room, and a kind of central hall where the space heater was located. A stick-built house is one where there are no prefabricated parts. The joists, the wall frames, and the rafters were all built one stick of wood at a time. The work was done in the evenings and on weekends. Before long, my father had his own place.

He couldn't afford to hire a company to drill a well, but he had a shovel. A hand-dug well requires a tremendous amount of work and an even greater amount of faith. My father used a divining rod to pick the place. A drilled well consists of a one-inch hole drilled in the ground and filled with a pipe. The hole is drilled as deep as necessary to provide the proper flow of water. A hand-dug well needs to start with a hole in the ground big enough around for a man to comfortably stand in, and dig in. The hole has to stay that large around, no matter how deep the well has to be. The fact is that water from a hand-dug well is sweeter than water from a drilled well.

My father hand-dug this well and built the well house.

My father's stick-built house and hand-dug well taught me the real value to things. It was a mansion. It was a castle. It was his. The real value was not in the amount of money that it cost. The real value was in the pride of labor. Every board that was cut, every nail that was driven, every piece of sheet rock that was hung, and every shovel full of dirt was a labor of love. Maybe every family, today, should be required to hand dig a well, especially in the hard-packed, red clay of Wake County.

Rick camps out in front of the house that his dad built by hand.

Practical Lessons

My father taught me his work ethic by example. It's a simple, but profound, philosophy. If you are going to be a supply room clerk, be the best supply room clerk you can be. Give more to your job than your boss expects. Don't ask for pay raises; earn them. If you excel at your job, you will be rewarded.

My father loved to stay busy. An idle hour was a wasted hour. That was the reason he had so many "other" jobs. Even though he put the extra income, which he received from all of the extra jobs to good use, I don't think he took on all those extras just for the money. He simply loved to work.

And working meant being on time. To be late for anything is a symbol of contempt. My father taught me the simple truth that being on time is an outward expression of responsibility and courtesy. To this day, I would rather be ten minutes early than one minute late. In fact, if I am going to be late, I would rather not go at all.

Even though my father had little formal education, he instilled in me the need to be educated. I was not a strong student. In fact, I didn't like school very much. I never went to college, but I did receive training in computer programming through ECPI College of Technology, and that training proved to be just what I needed to get my first full-time job. Though I didn't obey my father's direction, I did listen. I guess I was too stubborn to do what he wanted, but I was not too stubborn to learn. I am proud that my children are both college graduates. It just took an extra generation for this lesson to sink in. College is not for everyone. People who master a trade have also received an education.

My father taught me a lot, but my dad taught me even more.

Bird Hunting and Dialysis

It was my dad who took me bird hunting. There was just something about being out in the fields with him and the other men. I can't remember how old I was when he trusted me enough to carry a shotgun, but somehow I knew that only a dad would trust a child with a loaded gun.

It was my job to tend to the bird dogs. We had one particularly good pointer named "Cindy." Dad had trained her. It was an amazing thing to watch her work the field, and how Dad could control her with simple voice commands. It wasn't necessarily what Dad said to her, but the way in which he said it, that made Cindy so effective as a hunter and retriever.

My father controlled "Cindy" and his other dogs with simple voice commands.

My father had a stern, almost demanding voice. My dad had a caring, compassionate tone. Different tones meant different things.

My mother suffered from diabetes. Towards the end of her life, it became a debilitating disease. Three times each week, after retiring from the Division of Motor Vehicles, she would need dialysis. It was dad who rose to the occasion – who treated her with care, compassion, and concern.

As mom's illness progressed, my father was forced to rethink his priorities. Maybe working eighteen hours a day wasn't such a good idea after all. And the man who used to take me hunting came in from the fields and cared for his wife. There is something of eternal significance about a dad who shows his children a tender side.

Mom and Dad, just before Mom became ill.

My father was never one to show much affection to me. In fact, he would say that real men don't hug.

But my dad has a tender spot. When I went into politics, and throughout my political service, my dad saved every newspaper article that mentioned my name. He brought me four large boxes recently, each filled with clippings from the paper.

"I thought you might like to have these," he said quietly as he headed out the door to work at the flea market.

I can't remember, but I think we might have hugged. Thanks, Dad.

Chapter 4

On Being Cool (And Keeping My Cool)

"It is a shame that youth is wasted on the young."
—MARK TWAIN

Like every other teenage boy who ever lived, I wanted to be cool. But, I was far from cool. I was too tall, too heavy (I'm reluctant to use the word fat, even though that's the most accurate description), and too ugly (have you ever known a teenage boy who didn't think he was ugly?) to be cool. Most of the time, I wore a crew cut. I didn't particularly like the look, but my father did. Crew cuts were cheaper than any other hair cut. I wore braces and glasses – the late 1960's black plastic framed type. Nothing could be less cool.

I'm pretty sure that a big, fat guy looking for a way to be cool invented the game of football. It seemed like my only option, my only way to fit in. So I went for it.

Vaiden Whitley High School was no football machine. We never played for a championship. We were an average team – competitive in some games, blown away in others. We were an average team, and I fit right in. I was an average player.

I must have looked a little like a gentle giant. The shoulder pads, hip pads, kneepads, ankle braces, wristbands, pants, jersey, and helmet combined to give me a larger than life appearance. And since I was already larger than everybody else, the added weight and bulk of the pads at least made me look like a football player. Cool.

My high school picture. I'm glad I looked more "cool" in a football uniform.

I have heard some athletes sing the praises of football. It's the noble sport. It is supposed to teach the value of teamwork, the need for self-sacrifice, the desire to rise above defeat and conquer an opponent. It's controlled combat – a great battle of wills. Football is one-on-one competition within the larger game. It was all about hitting the other guy harder than he hits you. It's supposed to be a metaphor for life.

I suppose all of that is true, but what I remember most about football are two things: running and yelling.

Our coach believed in running. We might not be very good blockers, or tacklers, or passers, or catchers. But nobody was going to outrun us. Running laps began every practice. Laps were used to teach us discipline, and to discipline us. If we had a really good practice, we could end the practice with only three laps around the field, but each missed assignment would add a lap. I'm not sure we ever had a good practice.

Running. Running. Running. Running. Running. I could go on, but maybe you get the point. Running to the point of exhaustion. Running even after we were physically sick. Running in the dog days of August and in the freezing rain of November. Running on wobbly knees, carrying too much weight, with too many pads. And God forbid if any of us ever had the temerity to quit running and just finish the last lap by walking. Running was supposed to be teaching us enough discipline that we could please the coach. It was only after I injured my knee and couldn't play any more that I realized that Coach was never going to be pleased.

Since he wasn't pleased, Coach did a lot of yelling. Football may have been invented, not by a fat guy who wanted to be cool, but by a child abuser who wanted a legal way to abuse his victims. And with a whole team of boys who were constantly messing up, there was a lot to yell about. Football consists of 11 players on one side trying to execute a detailed play against 11 players on the other side determined to disrupt the plan. In every play there are winners and losers. In every play there are players who did their job and players who failed.

In every play there was somebody who could be yelled at and all of the coaches took advantage of the opportunity. I don't know if there is anything good about "in your face" confrontation. I'm sure that humiliation is never a good tactic. But both confrontation and humiliation were used on a regular basis.

I can't say that I enjoyed football, but I really enjoyed being cool. Not only was I cool, I learned to keep my cool. I learned that keeping my cool was a thousand times more important than being cool. The single most significant thing that playing football taught me was how to take criticism. It would come in pretty handy twenty years later when I entered politics.

Perception Isn't Really Reality

Football isn't the only activity in school where kids can be humiliated. Kids are unbelievably abusive to each other. Kids develop cliques and horribly abuse those kids who don't fit in. Big kids taunt little kids. White kids abuse black kids and black kids abuse white kids. Smart kids look down their noses at dumb kids. Popular kids humiliate the unpopular ones. There may be no more abusive place in the entire world than a middle school.

Sometimes, the teachers and administrators of a school get caught up in the abusing, and wittingly, or unwittingly become part of the problem. It happened to me when I was in the seventh grade.

I had braces put on my teeth earlier that year. There were the inevitable trips to the orthodontist for adjustments. Both my parents had bosses that would not let them off to take a child to the dentist, so my dad asked my Uncle George to take me. Uncle George was home on permanent disability so he had the time.

My Dad offered to pay Uncle George, but Uncle George refused the money.

"At least let me give you gas money," Dad said, but Uncle George said, "No."

Dad knew that Uncle George wouldn't take the money, at least not from him. Dad knew that Uncle George needed the money, and that he would take it from me. So each day that I had a trip to the orthodontist, my dad would give me $3 to give to Uncle George for gas.

Kids didn't take that kind of money to school in those days. Most kids carried just a quarter. That's what lunch cost. There was no need for any other money, because there wasn't anything to spend money on – there was a student store, but hardly anybody used it. Paper, pens, and rulers bought at the grocery store were a lot cheaper.

It was on one of the days that I was carrying my wad of money that I was humiliated. Some kid in my class went to the teacher and announced that he'd had $3 stolen from him.

I don't know if he really was telling the truth or not. It's possible that each of us happened to carry $3 to school that day, and that he really had lost his.

That's when the teacher got involved. She shut the door to the classroom, and announced that no one was leaving until she got to the bottom of this. She stood before the class and demanded that the guilty party return the money. It would go easier on the guilty party if he confessed. Nobody moved. Then she announced that she was going to do a student-by-student search.

Each of us, in turn, made our way to her desk. We were asked to empty our pockets, and to bring our book bags with us so she could search them as well.

When my turn came, I emptied my pockets – and there it was. The evidence! Three dollars, folded neatly, inside a note from my parents giving me permission to miss part of the school day.

"Why didn't you confess, when you had the chance?" she asked. "You're in a lot of trouble, young man!"

I was accused, tried, and convicted. And I was about to be sentenced. A trip to the principal's office was in store. As I was led out of the classroom, every eye was upon me. All of my classmates knew that I was a thief and a liar.

Just like the Duke Lacrosse players, many years later, I was branded. The perception was that I was guilty. The evidence pointed to my guilt. The accuser seemed genuine. I had the money; there couldn't be any other explanation. Except the truth.

Even though my parents went to school the next day and straightened everything out, life was never the same for me. Some of my classmates believed my story. Many did not. And there was always the perception...maybe his parents just bought off the principal and the teacher. Seventh graders have vivid imaginations.

Accusations are hurtful. Unfair accusations hurt even more.

"Hold your head up high," Mom said. "You didn't do anything wrong."

"But everybody thinks I did."

"Who cares what everybody else thinks?" she asked.

I cared. We all do. We want people to like us, to trust us, to love us. Perception isn't really reality, but it sure feels like it.

Life isn't fair. But it sure is interesting.

Chapter 5

Out of the Tobacco Fields

"Only fools idle away their time."
—PROVERBS 12:11 (NEW LIVING TRANSLATION)

I'm pretty sure that I never had a hobby, unless a rare trip to the fields to hunt birds counts as a hobby. We learn a lot from our dads, and since my dad was always working, I learned that working was the best way to spend our time – even our free time.

When my football playing days came to an end, I needed something to fill the void. After school, on weekends, and summers I worked. There were a variety of jobs. I often worked with my Dad in one of his many side businesses. We had a couple of office buildings and stores, which we cleaned at night. There was a carpet cleaning business. And there were the hot dog and hamburger grills.

I especially enjoyed working at the grill in Lizard Lick. Not only did we have a typical menu for a small country grill, but we also sold hand dipped ice cream. I'm convinced that I ate up all of the profit. I gained thirty pounds overnight. Each time I dipped ice cream for a customer, I'd dip some for myself. It was a tough job, but somebody had to do it.

I also worked outside the family business. There was a time when I worked as an attendant at a service station outside of Rolesville. In those days, gas stations really were service stations. The customers sat in their car while I pumped the gas. And while the tank was being filled,

I'd wash windshields (front and back), check the oil, check the air filter, check the water in the radiator, and check the air in the tires.

I enjoyed being a service station attendant, because as I was servicing their cars, I had a chance to talk with the customers. Talking with people is the one thing that I have always done naturally. And people seemed to enjoy talking with me. The art of conversation isn't so much an art as it is a gift. I had the gift of making people comfortable. It's amazing what people will tell a teenage service station attendant.

"Boy," the owner of the gas station told me one day, "you have a way with people."

To make extra money, I also worked for a used car salesman who financed the cars he sold. I don't think he ever took advantage of people by charging too much interest. He was just there to help people.

He would sell his cars (or make his loans) to folks "on time," with just a handshake on the details. People would come by the car lot to make their monthly or weekly payments. A little book in the bottom drawer of his desk was his official record. Because he had a steady stream of customers who were there to pay down their loan, he had to hang around the station nearly all the time.

When he saw how well I "got on" with "his people," he decided that I could be trusted to be a collector. He let his people know that I could take their payments and showed me how to record them in his little book.

People were not at all ashamed to borrow money from him. He was just an informal banker. And his business was based on trust. He loaned money based on a person's word. The banks required collateral. All he required was a handshake. Just as he trusted that the people he loaned money to would pay him, they trusted that he would give them a fair deal and keep an accurate account.

"Most people are good people," he told me once. "If you treat people with kindness and respect, you'll get kindness and respect in return."

It was kind of him to trust me. I wasn't about to let him down.

From Rolesville to Fort Jackson

I graduated from Vaiden Whitley High School in 1971. I wasn't college material. I may have had a gift for talking with people, but I had no gift for book learning. This is really strange to me, because I love to read, and even to this day I read everything I can related to running a small business or politics. Suffice it to say that my high school grades were not very good. I don't think I could have gotten into college.

There was a second, even larger, impediment to going to college. I couldn't afford it. My mom and dad couldn't afford it either. I guess if college had been a great dream of mine, they would have sacrificed, and Dad would have gotten a third (or fourth) job to help make it happen, but I wasn't interested. Besides, I had already exceeded my dad's level of education. He didn't graduate from high school and he had done pretty well for himself.

My high school graduation. Mom and Dad were really proud. I don't know why none of us were smiling.

As an 18 year-old, recent high school graduate, I hit the job market in the summer of 1971. It was an interesting year. America was at war. The Viet Nam War was beginning to wind down, but no one knew it for sure. The draft was still in effect, and the Selective Service had instituted a draft lottery to make things fair. The lower the number, the worse. My lottery number was 33. It was clear that I was headed to the Army.

I wasn't opposed to the war. I thought that our effort in Viet Nam was a noble one, maybe that's the real reason I didn't want to go to college. The colleges were all a hotbed of protest against the war. I knew that I wouldn't "fit in."

I wasn't eager to join the Army either. I guess I was hoping that the war would miraculously come to an end, or that the draft would be ended. I wasn't opposed to military service. In fact, I thought that serving in the military would be an honor, and that service to country was a good thing. I was a typical 18 year-old – I was confused. I set out to get a job, ignoring the fact that I had a draft number that virtually guaranteed that I would be called to military service. Two things became clear very quickly: I needed more than a high school education and nobody in their right mind was going to hire a kid who was about to be drafted.

If college was out, a trade school would have to be in. In the early 70's, it was clear to me that computers were the coming thing. Personal computers were a distant dream, but nearly every business was computerizing, so I headed to ECPI for a crash course in computer programming. It was a demanding course – four hours of class work every day for six months and homework every night. Computers use their own unique language. Computer programming is all about knowing and using the language to get the computer to do what you want it to do. Everyone who works with a computer today knows that computers do exactly what you tell them to do and not what you think you tell them to do.

I did a good job at ECPI. Maybe because I was paying for it, or maybe because I somehow knew that this was my ticket to a future, I was suddenly a good student, but it wasn't an easy six months.

I had moved on from the service station business to work at a Winn Dixie grocery store in Raleigh. I looked really spiffy in Winn Dixie's classic white shirt and red bow tie. Winn Dixie was glad to have me do my work on either second or third shift.

So every day from 8:00 a.m. to noon I attended ECPI. From noon to three, I began my homework. From three to 11:00 p.m., I worked at Winn Dixie. From midnight until I was finished I worked on homework. If I was lucky, I'd get three hours of sleep a night. The energy of an 18 year-old is amazing.

It was while I was working at Winn Dixie one night that my talking skills brought a great blessing. I was talking with a customer and we had a long discussion about life, about jobs, and about computers.

It was during this conversation that he mentioned that a large Midwest manufacturing company called Square D was moving to the area and would need computer programmers. The day I received my certificate from ECPI, I headed to the Square D recruiting office.

There was no question that Square D needed people. The plant was under construction. Workers of all types were needed, including computer programmers. Square D is a company which manufactures components for the electrical industry, and they were going to hire 1,000 people.

But the other problem was still there. I had a skill, but I also had a low draft number. No businessman wanted to hire someone, train him, and then lose him to the war. It was the personnel director at Square D that found the solution. If I would join the National Guard, when I completed basic training, a computer programming job would be waiting for me when I returned.

It seemed like the perfect solution – a six-year commitment to the Guard in exchange for a good job. Members of the Guard, after two months of basic training, were committed to serve one weekend a month and two weeks each summer for six years.

So I joined up. I met a bus in downtown Raleigh. I was told to bring nothing but what I was wearing and a small bag that I could ship those clothes home in. A country boy headed to Fort Jackson, South Carolina.

I looked really smart in my Army dress uniform.

When I arrived at Fort Jackson, it was football all over again – lots of yelling and lots of running, but somehow this was different.

War is a deadly serious business. And so is preparing for war. The drill sergeant had served three tours in Viet Nam, and he was determined to prepare each of us for what we might have to face. He yelled incessantly, was constantly in our faces, and berated us with never ending insults. Somehow, I didn't mind.

My dad, and everybody else who knew that I was headed to basic, gave me the same advice: keep your mouth shut, never volunteer for anything, and just blend in. I guess that's a way of saying that people skills are not very important in the early days of military training.

Listening is important. I did everything that I was told. I ran and ran and ran. When I was running in football practice, it was always drudgery. When I was running in basic, it was almost a joy. I ended up, like everybody else who finishes basic, in the best shape of my life.

I learned what everybody else learned. I learned respect; respect for authority, respect for my country, respect for myself, and respect for life. When you are training to kill others or be killed, you develop a great joy of living. Being prepared physically, mentally, and emotionally to stay alive makes every moment that you do live precious.

When basic was over, military life became more routine. Just as in real life, sometimes the military doesn't make sense. In my Advanced Individual Training (AIT), I was trained to be an office clerk. To be certified, I had to be able to type 20 words per minute. I passed my certification, barely, with the hunt and peck method. As soon as I was certified, I was assigned to the motor pool! I spent the next six years with my head under the hood of a jeep or truck.

I was assigned to the guard unit in Rocky Mount, North Carolina. As with any military unit, there was a lot of down time. We did a lot of sitting around, and a lot of talking. We generally hated the war protesters, not because of their stand on the war, but because of the hatred with which they protested. We hated them because of their hatred for us. As a unit, we all agreed that it would be better to have to go to Viet Nam than to face our fellow citizens in a protest that had turned violent. Fortunately, though we trained for both things, neither happened.

I was ready to bunk out in my fatigues.

When I finished basic training, I went to Square D to start my job as a computer programmer. My training had "taken too long" and "we had to fill that job" but "we are going to honor our commitment and give you a job as a fork lift operator."

I took the job. At least I had my foot in the door. Maybe I could work, or talk, my way into something better.

Chapter 6

Together As One

"A worthy wife is a husband's joy and crown!"
—PROVERBS 12:4

Sherry is beautiful. I am homely. (I'm not ugly, just not particularly handsome). She is tall, thin, and picturesque. I am overweight. She is well educated, a college graduate. She is cultured. I am a country boy. She is thoughtful, deliberate. I am rash, and impulsive. She is a saint more than a sinner. I am a sinner more than a saint.

From my point of view, we were a perfect match.

We met in late October of 1976 at a Square D management dinner. Sherry was a new employee who was to begin her employment in a few weeks as an industrial engineer. She had graduated from Meredith College with a double major in math and accounting. (Did I mention that she is smart?) We just hit it off! I have to admit, that I don't remember our first date. I was embarrassed about this until I asked her about it, and she couldn't remember either. We are growing older, I guess. We had a whirlwind romance, and were married the next November.

From my point of view, we are still a perfect match.

The wedding was everything that Sherry wanted which made both of us happy. We were married at the First United Church of Christ in Winston-Salem, North Carolina. It was an evening ceremony. All of the members of the wedding party were, of course, dressed in evening wear. Candles were everywhere. I don't remember much about the ceremony, except that it was long. That preacher prayed the longest prayers that I have ever heard. I guess he thought that I needed them. Prior to the wedding, we were scheduled to have five one-hour sessions of premarital counseling with the pastor. It was in the third of these sessions that the preacher told us that we were doing so well that we might not need the fourth and fifth sessions.

"But let me ask you one last question before you go," he said. "Rick. You've had a long, difficult day. On the way home from work you dream up an evening of fun and relaxation with Sherry. You walk in the door and announce your plans to her. Her response is complete refusal. What do you do?"

"Well," I said, "I have always heard that husbands need to put their foot down at some point, and I guess that is just what I'd do. I'd put my foot down!"

"That was absolutely the wrong answer!" the pastor said. "I'll see you next week."

It's a funny thing, to me, that I can remember that conversation, but not our first date. I never have put my foot down. If I had, it would probably have gotten stepped on. Fortunately, I have never felt the need.

Maybe it's because we were a perfect match.

After all these years, we still are. I know that Sherry is the best part of me. I love her more deeply each day.

Our love is bound up in mutual respect. I respect her wisdom, her thoughtfulness, her kindness and gentleness. I can honestly say that we have never had a shouting argument. When we disagree about something, we sit down and calmly discuss it. We listen to each other. I think I learned this from watching her parents interact with each other.

The mutual respect which they showed each other seemed like an incredibly strong foundation for building a great marriage. It worked for her parents, and it has worked for us.

Sherry is my best friend. Best friends talk. I can't imagine what a day would be like without a conversation with my best friend. It just wouldn't make sense. It would be like saying that you love God, but never praying with Him. It would be like planting a garden, but never tending it, or buying a new car and never driving it. I love to talk. It is, after all, one of my greatest strengths; being a people person is all about the ability to connect with someone through conversation. But most great talkers are not very good listeners. Through the years, Sherry has taught me when to shut up and listen. Though she doesn't talk as much as I do, when she does say something, it is always worth hearing.

I don't think that I have ever told her that she is my perfect soul mate. But I should. I hope that I have shown her; that I have returned her care with care, her love with love, her compassion with compassion.

She has done far more than I could ever do. She has supported me in my wild schemes and plans. She has rejoiced with me in my successes. She has held me close in times of defeat and despair. She has been my stabilizer – I tend to get out in right field when I'm supposed to be at first base. Sherry brings me home. I have many faults; I tend to get obsessed with work and working. Sherry reminds me of the more important things, like home and family and faith, and gently calls me home.

We are a perfect match, because she covers all my weakness and makes me know that when I am with her, I am home.

It is a fortunate man who can brag about his children after they have become adults. Sherry and I have two grown children, Jennifer and Kevin. They are both reflections of their mother's nurturing.

About the only roles I played in their "raising" was being the disciplinarian and, hopefully, passing on to them the work ethic that my Dad instilled in me.

The best two kids in the world, Kevin and Jennifer.

Before Jennifer was born, Sherry and I had mutually agreed that the job of mothering a child was far more important than any job in the corporate world. We agreed that living on one income instead of two was not a sacrifice, but a privilege and we would be "paid back" with memories that would last a lifetime, with children that we could be proud of, and with a legacy that would carry into eternity.

Sherry created a home. She taught our children, loved them, encouraged them, prayed with them, played with them, and corrected them – she was everything a mother was supposed to be. She was preparing them to do the one thing that every mom hates to see happen but knows is inevitable. She was preparing them to leave the nest and soar on their own.

Sherry and I always assumed that our kids would go to college. We talked with them about college from the first days that they entered elementary school. A college education was a "given." Jennifer sailed through high school at Cardinal Gibbons. During her senior year, we went on a tour of colleges and universities and she fell in love with Furman, a Baptist related university in South Carolina. It was the only school to which she applied and was accepted in the early admission program. She graduated with honors with an accounting degree, having been awarded both of the special awards presented to graduates of the School of Accounting. She then went on to North Carolina State University and received a master's degree in accounting. Jennifer is smart, like her mom, but her good grades didn't come easy; she had to work at them. I am proud that no challenge was ever too big for her. If she needed to work hard to accomplish a goal, that simply made the accomplishment sweeter.

Kevin is gifted. He could probably make all A's and never open a book, but he was never particularly interested in scholarship. As a teenager, he had two great passions: being outdoors and tinkering with cars. Being a Boy Scout was perfect for him. He loved camping, fishing, hunting and anything to do with the outdoors. He earned his Eagle Scout award by the time he was sixteen. If there had been a higher award then Eagle, he would have pursued it. He also loved anything mechanical. When he was fifteen, he talked me into buying him an old Camaro so he could work on it. He tinkered. He piddled. He learned. And he fell in love. Auto mechanics was a natural gift. Some years later, he bought a small pickup truck with a four-cylinder engine. He took the souped-up engine out of the Camaro, modified the engine compartment of the truck and installed the Camaro engine, and made all of the changes in the transmission that were necessary to make the conversion work. He had one powerful small truck.

Kevin talked a lot about being an auto mechanic. I told him that he could become a mechanic, but only after he received a college degree. I even promised him that I would send him to any auto mechanics training school that he wanted to attend, but only after he had received an undergraduate degree. He graduated from North Carolina State with a degree in tourism management and a minor in business.

Both Kevin and Jennifer got good jobs after graduating. And though they were both doing well in their professions, it is a pleasant irony to me that they are both now working in the family business. Both of them have come home to work with me in the furniture store.

Sherry created such a wonderful home that our children flew right back to it. It couldn't make me happier.

Rick, Sherry, Jennifer, and Kevin at home together.

Chapter 7

Selling Fleas - Big & Small!

"He that is good at making excuses is seldom good for anything else."

—BENJAMIN FRANKLIN

Square D is a large manufacturing company that makes equipment for the electrical industry. The home office of the company is in Illinois. In the early 1970's, the company made a decision to open a large facility in the South and the little town of Knightdale, North Carolina was chosen as the site. Knightdale is about fifteen miles from Raleigh.

In 1971, when I came on board as a forklift operator, the plant building had just been completed, but the facility was not yet operational. Every day, equipment and supplies would arrive from the company's Milwaukee plant. It was my job to assist unloading all of the trucks which came to the site and distribute the various parts to whatever section of the plant needed them.

I really enjoyed having a full-time job. Even though it wasn't in the area where I had been trained, I took my Dad's advice and worked harder than anybody else. Being a forklift operator gave me the opportunity to learn about every aspect of the plant. As I delivered the various parts and supplies that were needed to get a major manufacturing plant up and running, I asked the obvious questions. "What does this machine do? How are these parts used? What does this department do?" I listened and learned. It wasn't long before I was a forklift operator who knew too much and I was promoted to be a production coordinator in the production control department.

Your Excuses Are Interesting, But I'm Not Interested in Your Excuses

It was in production control that I learned one of the most important business lessons of my life.

In the production control office, we were responsible to take orders from customers, sequence the orders, and provide, purchase, or manufacture the parts that were necessary to meet the orders. All customers were given a promised due date, and come hell or high water, the promises were to be fulfilled. Like all manufacturers, the company had production quotas which needed to be met. The company took great pride in being able to fulfill the special orders of customers, even though these orders had to be worked in to the regular orders.

My boss held weekly meetings with the various members of his staff. The purpose of these meetings was simple – he was checking to see if we were doing our jobs. In one of these weekly meetings, I went prepared with a long list of reasons why the promised due date for a large special order just couldn't be met. Whoever had taken the order and given the date was just unrealistic. My job was to see that promises of delivery were fulfilled, but there were just too many obstacles.

I told my boss, and the others who were at the production meeting, all the reasons why the promise was unrealistic. I thought I had done a pretty good job of explaining the situation. My boss asked to see me after the meeting. It was in this face-to-face encounter that I learned my lesson.

"You have a lot of excuses," he said. I started to protest. But he held up his hand to stop me, looked me square in the eye, and in a gentle and quiet voice said, "Your excuses are very interesting, but I'm not interested in your excuses."

Don't you just hate it when people yell at you quietly? And isn't it even worse when they are right? I have never understood why my boss decided to confront me quietly and alone instead of loudly and in the group meeting, but I appreciated it. His purpose was not to embarrass me but to teach me something. It worked.

I went back to my desk and asked myself all the "Why?" and "Why not?" and "How can we do it?" questions I could think of. The purpose of my asking the questions was not to seek more excuses, but to find the solutions that were necessary. I realized that I had spent as much, or more, time formulating all of the reasons why the promise couldn't be met than I needed to find the solution.

I spent twenty years in production control, inventory control, and manufacturing supervision at Square D. It was twenty years of no excuses.

That one confrontation turned me from passive to aggressive. It taught me the incredible value of asking the "why" questions. Reverend Billy Graham has said that the seven words, which killed more churches than any other words were "We've never done it that way before." The same could be said of any business, or any family, or any country. Asking the "why" questions for the purpose of seeking a better way is the key to success. Asking the "why" questions for the purpose of seeking excuses for change is the key to failure.

Have you ever been part of a dying business? Sometimes, they are hard to spot, because "the way things have always been done" has been pretty effective and an "if it's not broke, don't fix it mentality" takes hold. Such businesses are doomed to die. Get out before the funeral.

I'm not advocating change for change's sake. I am advocating change that solves the problems, change that creates new vision, change that produces hope, change that results in progress. The public schools are always recycling old ideas with new names. Nothing really changes, because to change would require answering all the "why" and "why not" questions which plague the public schools. Pouring more and more money into the schools hasn't worked, because, at the heart of the matter, no one has been forced to explain the excuses. I'm not advocating change for change's sake. I am advocating change that solves the problems, change that creates new vision, change that produces hope, change that results in progress.

Flea Market Fun

I had twenty good years at Square D. Because of my work ethic, and my drive to find the right answers to the "why" questions, I steadily advanced from forklift operator to third shift plant senior supervisor.

I had set a goal, very early in my life, to be making as much money as my dad made annually by the time I was twenty-one. With my base pay and the amount of overtime that I worked to help get the new plant up and running, I met the goal! Having money was wonderful. Being able to buy things was rewarding – the brand new 1975 Pontiac LeMans, motorcycle and dune buggy were "hot" – and buying my first house when I was only twenty-one was wonderful. But, there was something more rewarding than things.

I discovered that just being able to purchase something was reward enough. If I didn't really need the thing, just knowing that I *could buy it if I wanted to* was enough to satisfy me. I learned that family was more important than money, good neighbors were more important than a bigger house, relationships were more important than the latest gadgets.

The work ethic that I had received from my Dad was such a part of me that I had to be working more than one job. Throughout my days at Square D, I always had some kind of extra job. I didn't need the money; I had a need to be working. This compulsion to never have an idle hour led me to accept my dad's invitation (I still don't say "no" to him) to go into the flea market business.

It began innocently enough. My dad was sitting in a store in downtown Rolesville one afternoon "jawing" with some of the other town fathers. Downtown Rolesville was beginning to die. A shopping center was built out on the edge of town and most of the mom and pop stores downtown were closed or in the process of closing. They weren't moving to the new shopping center, they were just going out of business. One of the businesses that had been closed for a long time was the old livery stable, known by some of the locals as the Mule Stable. One of the grocery stores was already gone, and the other was on the way out. People had given up on Rolesville.

I don't know if it was my father or one of the other men who said, "Somebody ought to do something with that beautiful old building," referring to the stable. But it was definitely my dad who said, "It would be a great place for a flea market."

A dream was born. An idea was hatched. And that very day, Dad had entered into an agreement with the owner of the stable to turn it into a flea market. The building may have been beautiful in its early days. It was built with heart pine lumber – the floors were three inch thick tongue and groove pine. The post and beam construction held up the hay loft and supported the stalls in which mules would be bedded down for the night. Each stall had a wooden window that could be opened to allow the mule to stick his head out and see what was happening in Rolesville. Half of the building had no floor, but was a drive through where mule-pulled wagons would be driven through and loaded with fertilizer for those who tended their own mules back at the farm. This beautiful old building was unused, empty, falling into disrepair, and just perfect for an old fashioned flea market.

Herb Eddins sits and waits for customers outside his flea market.

A Fast Nickel Over A Slow Dime

My dad needed something to sell in his flea market. So, he went into the business of showing up at every yard sale he could and buying every small collectible he could find. He was also interested in buying any piece of good, used furniture that was available. His goal was to fill his pickup truck full every Saturday morning. It's amazing how much stuff you can get on a pickup truck, especially small collectibles. It wasn't long before Dad came to me and convinced me that two people out yard selling would be twice as productive as one.

So every Saturday morning, I would handle all of the yard sales in Raleigh that I could get to, and Dad would go to all of the ones out in the country. There were some simple keys to being a successful yard sale purchaser – be first on site; map out a plan and never backtrack, go to multiple family or neighborhood yard sales first, negotiate the price to get a better bargain (but don't waste time in bargaining), and purchase items in good condition. Worn out items at a yard sale will be worn out items in a flea market.

It was very early in the process that Dad and I learned that the most successful items for a flea market were "historic" collectibles (like those you see hanging on the walls at the Cracker Barrel restaurants) and really good used furniture. People who were moving, especially those who were downsizing often had really nice furniture that they simply didn't have room for. Good used furniture would sell almost as soon as we put it on the floor of the flea market. We discovered that incomplete sets (a dinette set with three chairs instead of four, or just one end table for instance) were hard to sell.

The word spread that the flea market in Rolesville was a good place to find furniture. I have always said "I will take a fast nickel over a slow dime" any day. By that, I mean that if the price is right, you don't have to wait for the right customer to come along. Every customer will potentially be the right customer. Interestingly enough, we never even had a "flea market" sign. Our business was built with happy customers sharing with their neighbors. They had come to the flea market and gotten a good deal. As people came to look at our furniture selections, over and over again they would say, "We wish you had new furniture, too." One day, in response, I said to myself, "Why don't we have new furniture?" I had made a horrible mistake – I had asked myself the "why" question. The answer seemed obvious.

Rolesville Furniture Store was about to be born.

Chapter 8

Bureaucracy Galore

"If Patrick Henry thought taxation without representation was bad, he should try it with representation."
—OLD FARMER'S ALMANAC

There was one very practical reason that running a furniture business in an old livery stable wouldn't work – there just wasn't room. It's a very simple thing that furniture that is on display takes up a lot of floor space and furniture that is not on display takes a lot of storage space.

When customers at our flea market asked that we begin to sell new furniture, it seemed like a good idea. I went to High Point and bought one truckload of furniture. I personally delivered the furniture back to the flea market, pushed aside some of the items that were already on the floor and disposed of some others, and put the new furniture on display. All of it sold almost over night.

For a couple of years, I made weekly runs to High Point. I would buy a pickup truck load of furniture, put it on display, and when it sold, head back to High Point for another load.

The flea market was located in downtown Rolesville. There was nothing architecturally pleasing about the buildings which made up downtown, but the buildings had what locals call "character." They were old. They were nondescript. They were structurally sound but needed a very good cleaning. They were a collection of country stores.

I decided that I could add to the "character" of downtown and meet one of my greatest needs at the same time. I would simply move another couple of old buildings onto the site. One of the first buildings that I moved to the site was an old train station that had been located in the Town of Zebulon. Since it was built around the same time as the livery stable (about 1900), it had the same "character" – an all wood, boxy structure. I moved the building into place behind the flea market, and it fit right in. It became the first of fourteen buildings that now make up Rolesville Furniture.

Herb calls to passersby from the window of the flea market.

It was when I attempted to move the third building into place that I ran into trouble. I had purchased an old store located at the county line and gone to the town office to get the proper permits. I had contracted with the mover to move the building. He had jacked it up off its old foundation, placed it on a special chassis, and hauled it to Rolesville. When the building arrived, someone from the town office came and informed me that I did not have the proper permits. The mover would not be allowed to complete the job.

It seems that some local citizen objected to the "character" of the buildings that I was placing in downtown. I had the permit which the town had issued, but I was informed that it wasn't valid. I had failed to cross some "t" or dot some "i." I didn't understand; I had the permit, but the permit wasn't good enough.

Numerous phone calls and what seemed like hundreds of meetings later, the building was sitting by the side of the road on its chassis, the town was fining me approximately $100 a day, the mover was charging me a "daily usage fee" for the chassis, and nothing was being resolved. A meeting was held with representatives of the town of Rolesville, me, and representatives of all of the various inspections departments for Wake County. The impasse had become so difficult that the head of the department of inspections was present.

During the meeting, the various departments were discussing among themselves about whose part of the permitting process was more important, and what the timing of the various parts should be. It was clear to me that I was caught in the middle of a bureaucratic and political tug-of-war. The town wanted one thing, the county another, and I wanted something else. It may have been the single most frustrating meeting that I have ever attended. Apparently, every step that I had taken with the town to get the original permit had been the wrong step, and every step that I had taken to resolve the problem had simply made the problem worse. At some point in the process, I put my head down on the desk. It was an outward expression of the futility that I felt and utter exhaustion.

When I laid my head on the table, the arguing bureaucrats suddenly stopped talking. Silence really is golden.

"You've had all you can handle, haven't you?" the head of inspections said. I raised my head and nodded. I don't think that I even had the strength to answer. Then the most amazing thing happened, the bureaucrats and the politicians realized that they had gone too far.

"This meeting is over," he announced. Then he turned to me and said, "Rick, you come to my office, and I'm going to walk you through the whole process. We're going to start over, and we're going to do it right. I'm going to send you to the right people, in the right order, and we're going to straighten this whole thing out."

He did exactly what he said he would do. He not only sent me to the right people, but he had obviously prepared them for my coming. The whole process was handled quickly, efficiently, and with courtesy. It made me realize something about politics and government – politics and government can be incredibly frustrating if the politicians or the bureaucrats are fighting among themselves and the little guys get caught in the middle; but politicians and bureaucrats can also be incredibly helpful to the little guy. Everything depends on whether politicians are guarding their turf or fighting to do what is right.

I never moved another building to downtown Rolesville. I simply bought most of downtown. It seemed like good business, and politics was never involved.

Later, when I went into politics, I tried to remember what it was like to be the little guy who was caught in the middle, and I tried to remember the bureaucrat who turned out to be a nice guy once the turf battle was called off.

Other than church politics, small town politics may be the worst. Because everybody knows everybody else, much of small town politics is done in secret, behind the scenes. It's often called backstabbing. It's the most insidious form of politics, because you don't really know who to fight.

"They" don't want something done. "They" think it's a bad idea. "There are some people," "or "important" people who "prefer things be done a different way."

The problem in small town politics is that you often don't know who "they" are. It is, to be truthful, usually only one person of influence who doesn't want his name linked to that "dirty business of politics," but still wants to get his way.

If only good people of good will would just sit down and talk things out. That's a radical idea. It's what America's Founding Fathers envisioned congress doing. Unfortunately, most politicians have lost the goodwill part.

Chapter 9

The Rolesville Dream

"A man who is diligent in business will stand before kings and be served by other men."
—PROVERBS 22:29 (REVISED STANDARD VERSION)

Rolesville Furniture Company is a mom and pop furniture store and a very successful family business. When I left Square D to run the furniture store full time, it was one of the happiest and scariest moments of my life. I had grown use to a regular monthly paycheck. I had grown use to the security that having a full-time, good-paying job brings, but I was happy because I was fulfilling a dream to own and operate my own business.

Rolesville Furniture has grown to become a very large store. We occupy fourteen buildings on two of the corners of "downtown" Rolesville. All together, we have more square footage than most of the large furniture stores that dot the landscape of big cities, but we don't have an impressive showroom. We also don't have the overhead that the big stores have. As each of the small buildings that made up the heart of Rolesville became available, I bought them, usually at a nominal cost, and added them to my real estate empire.

There's nothing beautiful about Rolesville Furniture… until you walk in the door. We have made a very successful business by overcoming all of the odds. We have overcome a less-than-impressive facility with great prices. Simply put, we always have prices that are lower than our competition! The result is that the store has thrived.

In my years in the furniture business, I have learned some valuable lessons – lessons, which I'm going to pass on to you. These are commonsense things that anyone who is running a business or about to start one should know. But the fact is that I regularly beat my competition, probably because they haven't learned these lessons.

Persistence is more important than brilliance.

Every day there are roadblocks to succeeding. Don't let them defeat you. No one has ever accused me of being brilliant, but no one has ever outworked me. Persistence is that combination of stubbornness and faithfulness to a task that every successful person has.

We never trip over a mountain. When we face a mountain, we simply figure out a way of going over it, or around it, or tunneling through it. It's the little things, which are stumbling blocks, and it's the little things, which can stop our momentum. Little things like:

- Being too tired
- Not have enough education
- Being full of excuses
- Not knowing enough
- Having somcone else to blame

All of these things are just excuses. They may all be legitimate reasons for you not to succeed. Or, they may just be stumbling blocks that can be overcome with a little old fashioned persistence.

Productivity Determines Profitability

Productivity is determined by the utilization of *all of the resources* that you have. If you don't have the resources that you need, go and get them! To be profitable, you need to use your resources in an efficient and effective way.

Big companies can afford little mistakes, but not big ones. Years ago, the Zenith Corporation invested heavily in a new format that they were sure was the coming thing. It was a ceramic disc the size of an old LP record on which movies could be played. The discs required a special player that would be attached to a TV. At the same time that Zenith was investing heavily in this new technology, RCA invested in something new called a VCR. Zenith made a huge mistake. When was the last time you saw a Zenith TV? And have you ever seen a ceramic disc player?

Since even big businesses can be crippled by a big mistake, think what could happen to a small business that makes a big mistake. Small businesses don't have the financial backing to make big mistakes. That's why small businesses need to learn from the mistakes of other small businesses.

If you want to be profitable, be productive. Use every resource that you have to make your business stronger. At Rolesville Furniture, one of our resources is our space. We utilize every square inch for displaying furniture. The second a piece is sold, it is replaced. The more furniture we have displayed, the more we sell.

Be Passionate about Your Vision or Fail

Have you ever looked through a pair of binoculars the wrong way? It makes everything smaller. That's what happens when you surround yourself with the wrong kind of people. If you are going to be a successful businessman, you need to have people around you who will say "Yes!" to your ideas.

I don't mean "yes men." I mean people who can share your vision, see the dream, and realize the unfulfilled potential. One of the worst things that a person seeking success can do is surround himself with "no" people.

"No" people are folks who let the facts get in the way of faith, who see all of the possible downside of things, who are convinced that it just can't work. "No" people will rob you of your passion and, ultimately, destroy your vision.

Every good businessman needs someone who can keep him from going too far off the deep end. Usually that person is his banker. But good bankers are good dreamers, too. They lend money to people they are convinced are going to make money.

Do you have a great idea? Go for it! Passionately or not at all. And, be just as passionate about the day-to-day stuff. Look for new ways of doing that stuff better, get better systems, invest in new products, and find a new niche. If you need to expand, expand! Nike's ads say "Just do it!" I would add, "with passion!"

A Strong Business Can Run Without You

It might take years for you to develop a small business that is strong enough to run itself without you, but that should be your goal. I know you want to keep your finger on the pulse of everything that is going on, but if you do that, you will always have a small business.

It is essential that you develop people that you can trust. Train them to do their job and one other person's job – yours. And then, trust them.

If you are blessed to have someone on your staff that you already trust, show them! I am so glad that my Aunt Lillian, who is like a second mom to me, was already working for me at Rolesville Furniture when I first got elected to the House. She took on the responsibility of running the entire business while I pursued my political responsibilities. Lillian has a heart of gold. I was so glad that she was on board with the business and that I could trust her completely to take over and run things. Rolesville Furniture would not have grown into the business that it is today without her.

After you have trained others to do your job and theirs, you will be free to go and start another business, or expand the one you have in ways that you had never dreamed possible when you had to keep your finger on the pulse, or even go into politics.

Every Customer Should Leave Smiling

Are you too important, too busy to greet your customers? Then you're too busy! I personally greet most of the customers who come into our store.

"How are you today?" I ask.

"Fine," they say. "How are you?"

"Better than I deserve."

My answer almost always catches them off guard. It almost always makes them smile. I get a lot of interesting responses, everything from "Me too" to "Isn't God good?" I have discovered that if I can get them to smile on the way in the store, I am much more likely to have them smiling when they leave the store. If you can get people to smile with you, even laugh with you, you build a bond of trust.

I've always had the philosophy that I'll take a fast nickel over a slow dime any day. I take great pride in offering my customers the best furniture at the lowest possible prices. I take great pride in being able to save people money. It makes them smile, and me, too.

Existing Customers Are the Best Potential Customers

We don't spend a lot of money, as I said earlier, on fancy buildings and parking lots. I am sure that there are some people who come to our store who find it junky or too crowded with furniture. There are some customers who don't like to leave one building and have to go outside to enter another building, or even have to go across the street to find what they are looking for.

We can't please everyone. And we don't try. Our store would not appeal to the customer who wants to be able to say, "I bought the most expensive furniture I could find. I simply wanted the best." And our store would not appeal to the customer who wanted to see a whole room of furniture displayed just as it would be in her home.

But the customers we do appeal to come back. And they bring (or send) their friends. Not long ago, there was a lady parked outside our store with Illinois license plates on her car. She had been sitting in her car for a long time, talking on a cell phone. I walked by just as she was finishing her phone call.

"Are you all right?" I asked. "You seem lost."

"I've just moved here from Chicago," she said. "My mom sent me here to look for furniture. I'm used to really big furniture stores. When I got here, I just couldn't believe that this was the right place, so I called her to ask."

"Come on in and see," I said. She did, and she left smiling. She came because her mother sent her. She'll send her new North Carolina friends. And, she'll be back.

Be Bold, Not Stupid

Existing customers are great, but they are not enough. New customers are always needed. Some old customers die; some move away. New customers are essential to the health of any business.

But how do you get them? By being bold.

I recently read in the local paper that there is a car dealer in the area who has a nine million dollar annual TV advertising budget. Nine million dollars! For that car dealer, with the incredible amount of money invested in car lots and showrooms and the cars themselves, a nine million dollar advertising budget makes sense. It's bold, but not stupid.

Sometimes, it's hard to know when you are about to cross the line between boldness and stupidity. But it won't take long to find out. If you have never done anything stupid, you probably haven't done anything particularly bold either.

One of the most stupid things that a businessman can do is not be bold enough. Being cautious costs more money than being bold.

Most of my boldness comes in my advertising. When I first started advertising, I didn't see hardly any results. I was about to give up on advertising all together when I decided to compare my ads (which had been designed by the newspaper staff) with all of the other ads in the paper. They were all alike. My ad didn't stand out at all. From that moment, I made the decision to start designing my own ads. I didn't know anything about advertising, but the advertising department at the paper didn't know anything about my business either. Laid out by a non-professional, my ads were different! And they began to work.

Since advertising is expensive and you can only expect to get about a two percent return, I decided to do something even bolder. Most businesses decide to have a sale, set their prices, and then advertise the sale date and prices. I do it the opposite. I write a fantastic ad – what would I want to see if I was a customer – and then set my prices to meet the ad. That's either very stupid or very bold. All I know is, it works.

Good Results Are the Enemy of Great Results

One of the greatest enemies of a really successful business is contentment. It is so easy to fall into the trap of "if it ain't broke, don't fix it." If it ain't broke, it still needs tuning.

Be fresh. Be creative. Kick it up a notch. Try something new. Go for greatness. Jesus said we wouldn't be good enough until we were holy and perfect (Matthew 5). Jesus probably would have been a good businessman.

Procrastination Is Our Greatest Enemy

Idle moments are wasted moments. Time is the one gift you can never get back and if you are not using it to go forward, you are going backward.

Remember that your competition is not sitting idly by hoping that you will fail so that they can pick up the pieces. Your competition is working hard. You have to work harder.

Never Compromise Virtue

Not long ago, one of my competitors sent his wife to our store to buy something. She bought a bedroom suite, and we delivered it to her home. When the delivery man got there, she told him to "just put it in the garage."

Later that day, my competitor called the manufacturer and accused him of selling his furniture to me cheaper than he was to him. When the manufacturer assured him that he was selling the furniture at the same price to both of us, my competitor didn't believe him. The manufacturer then called me and asked if I had intentionally underpriced the furniture because I was selling to my competitor's wife.

I told him, "No. I gave her the same deal I give everybody else."

There is absolutely no substitute for virtue. It is better to earn an honest living than to live dishonestly.

So there you have it. It's a simple list of commonsense things that anyone can do to succeed in business. I'm not much worried about my competition doing all these things and taking business away from me. If they do, there is plenty of business out there for all of us. If they don't, there's just more business for me.

The fact is that most people know these things, but just don't do them. The ninety-eight percent of the people who don't do them end up working for the two percent of the people who do.

Chapter 10

Call from God: Just Listen & Act

"Here I am, Lord. Send me."
—ISAIAH 6:8 (NEW AMERICAN STANDARD)

I don't remember a word of the sermon, or even the altar call, but I found myself at the altar rail. I had been called by God, not to be a preacher or a prophet, but simply to be a child of His.

The pastor greeted me. I told him of my desire to be born again, to become a new person in Christ. He was thrilled and invited me to meet with him later that week to discuss the implications of my answering a call from God.

It was in our meeting that the pastor explained to me the significance of the Blood of the Lamb. Christ had shed His blood for me! It's an astonishing thing when faith moves from being a corporate and intellectual thing to being a personal and heartfelt experience. I experienced the personal touch of God. I knew that I had, indeed, been saved.

Even though I am now a United Methodist, I was raised a Baptist, a Southern Baptist. Southern Baptists put a lot of emphasis on "being saved." Southern Baptists teach and preach that the unsaved are going to hell, that they deserve it, and that the only way to avoid the just punishment for sin is to trust in Jesus as Savior. I believed. With every core of my being, I believed.

My belief needed to be confirmed and celebrated in the church. Baptists do this through believer's baptism, an immersion into water which recreates the death and burial of Christ and His resurrection into new life. My baptism took place on a Sunday morning at Wake Crossroads Baptist Church when I was 16 years old. I can honestly say that I have been a believer ever since.

I love the Lord. But I have struggled with the church. The problem with the church is that it is made up of people – people like me. I confess that I have drifted away from the church. I have fallen into the sin of being content with my faith, and have even been known to make the statement that you don't have to go to church to be a Christian. I didn't make a decision to leave the church. I wasn't mad. I was just frustrated and weary. I have grown weary with the few people (every church has them) who constantly ruffle feathers, the few people who feel the need to be stirring the pot, the few people who fight over every trivial matter. Church committees and boards can fight for ages over trivial things that ultimately mean absolutely nothing – the color of the carpet, or whether or not we clap in church – but never discuss the core issues of the faith, like whether or not the Gospel is being presented to the lost. It is a great irony to me that I love politics outside of the church and hate it inside of the church.

Even though I am not as active a church goer as I should be, I have never lost my faith. There have been great trials in my life, but I have never doubted. I have joined every true believer in questioning God sometimes, in wondering why He does what He does, and why His timing and my timing don't always seem to mesh up, but I have never stopped believing.

My faith in a God who calls us into relationship with Him and into His service is every bit as strong today as it was when I was sixteen. God speaks to people who are willing to listen.

The story of Elijah, the Old Testament prophet, is my story. Elijah was tired. He had given every ounce of his strength in defeating the 850 prophets of the Baal's, the false gods. The next day, Elijah heard that the evil Jezebel, who was a believer in the Baals, was out to kill him. Elijah, the great man of God, ran away in fear. He went into hiding in a cave on Mount Horeb and waited forty days and forty nights to hear God speak. God announced to Elijah that He was about to pass by, and Elijah went to the mouth of the cave to watch.

"Then a great and powerful wind tore the mountain apart and shattered the rocks, before the Lord, but the Lord was not in the wind. After the wind there was an earthquake, but the Lord was not in the earthquake. After the earthquake came a fire, but the Lord was not in the fire. And after the fire came a gentle whisper. When Elijah heard it, he pulled his cloak over his face." (I Kings 19: 11-13)

The gentle whisper, or small voice, is with us still. The voice speaks in our consciences, and everybody has a conscience. Some of us are well practiced at ignoring the whisper and we are all guilty of wondering if the voice we hear is really God.

But sometimes, God breaks through. I had been thinking about running for the Raleigh City Council for several weeks. It didn't make any sense. After all, my dad had said to me over and over again, "When you become a man, work hard, keep your nose clean, and never, ever get involved in politics." What was I thinking? I had never served on any government committee. I had no knowledge of how the city council worked, or what I might want to accomplish if I got elected. In fact, other than voting, I had never been involved in government in any way.

One morning, about 5:30 a.m., I woke suddenly. I was wide awake, and the first thought on my mind was the city council. I got out of bed. In those days, before Hurricane Fran tore it down, we had a gazebo out in the backyard. I felt compelled to go to the gazebo, even though I hardly ever sat there. As the day dawned, as the darkness fled in the face of the new day, I knew that God was calling me into politics. There was no great, thundering voice. There was just a gentle whisper, an assurance that this stupid thing I was about to do was a calling. I knew that God would be with me and that in being a politician, I would be serving God.

When Sherry woke up later that morning, I told her about my decision. I figured if she didn't support me, then I would just ignore the whole thing. I would put it down to just being a crazy idea. But she did support me. She even agreed to work on my "campaign." I went to the Board of Elections and paid the filing fee to put my name on the ballot for City Council.

I was a Southern Democrat. Southern Democrats were not like the Democratic Party of today. Southern Democrats were culturally and fiscally conservative. In those days, the State of North Carolina was still a mostly Democratic state. The Republican Party was beginning to make some inroads, but the Democrats truly controlled the state government.

I called the state Democratic headquarters, told them I was running for the Raleigh City Council, and asked for their help. Their only help was to say something like, "Good luck." They offered no advice, no support, and certainly no financial support. I was on my own. I later learned that they were supporting two other candidates in the race. It made me mad. Maybe I wasn't a Democrat after all. Even before Election Day, I changed my party affiliation to Republican.

I didn't know anything about running a campaign. I had no organization, hardly any money, no experience, no name recognition. But I had a calling. I was pretty sure that God was going to see to it that I won.

I lost. I came in third. I lost big.

At first, I couldn't understand it. Why would God call me to get involved in the race and then let me lose? Had I been wrong? Was it only the birds singing and the wind rustling that morning in the gazebo? Then it dawned on me – God may have called me to enter the race, but He didn't promise to run the race for me. God calls us to all kinds of tasks. But He doesn't do for us what we are capable of doing for ourselves. Miracles occur when people of faith do all that they can and trust God to do the things they can't do.

Even though I lost, I had been bitten by the political bug. And, I had caught the eye of some local Republican politicians. They came to me and urged me to run for the North Carolina Legislature. I agreed to run, knowing that I would have some help this time, and knowing that I would never be outworked by an opponent again. I won a seat representing northern Raleigh, the Wake Forest and Rolesville areas.

Is God involved in politics? I surely hope that He is. In fact, the Book of Romans says, "There is no government authority except those whom God has established." (13:1) In our separation of church and state society, we are suspicious of people who run for office publicly while waving the Bible about. If a politician was to say that he was "listening to the voice of God and following His will," he would never be elected. But if a politician was to say the opposite, "I don't believe in prayer," he wouldn't be elected, either. We are a schizophrenic society.

God was always involved in my political life. He didn't direct me, or tell me how to vote. He didn't support my side against the other side. He didn't send me buckets of money to run campaigns. But He was involved.

God was involved, because I am a believer. Not only do Christians believe that God has saved us, but that He will also judge us. I believe that, one day, I will be standing before the throne of God. I will have to answer for every vote that I made, every compromise that I entered into, every bill that I introduced or failed to introduce.

God is going to look me in the eye and ask, "Did you fulfill that calling I gave you?' I want to be able to, without any reservation, answer "Yes," and to hear Him reply, "Well done."

I know that politics can be a dirty business, but there is also integrity in politics. Every member of the legislature must be a person of integrity. If one member of the House or Senate makes an agreement with another member, and then breaks that agreement, he or she has lost all credibility. The word spreads like wildfire. If you can't be trusted, as a member of the legislature, your effectiveness is destroyed. Such members need to pack their bags and go home!

I am a conservative Republican. On most social issues I swing to the right, sometimes to the far right. I am also a person of faith. I was acquainted with many liberal Democrats who swung to the left on social issues, sometimes far left, who were also persons of faith. I believe that they were as sincere in their beliefs as I was in mine. Politics, at its best, is the art of winning the hearts and minds of the people. Surely God is involved in that.

The house chamber was like a sanctuary to me. There was a hallowedness about the place. And God was watching.

Chapter 11

Shots Fired - One Dead at Home

"You shall not murder."
—EXODUS 20:13 (NEW AMERICAN STANDARD)

It was one of those phone calls that you never want to get. There had been a murder in the family.

In his retirement, my Uncle Claude had taken over managing a small trailer park near his house. The most important part of managing was to collect the monthly rent from the tenants. Most of the people who lived in the park paid their rent in cash, so on collection day Uncle Claude would have plenty of cash at the house.

I suppose everybody in the area knew that at least once a month Uncle Claude would be rich, even though the money wasn't his. There were a couple of small time hoodlums in the area who decided that they would rob Uncle Claude.

He was, after all, an old guy. He wouldn't cause them any trouble. So the two guys went out and bought brass knuckles so that it would be easier to persuade Uncle Claude to part with the cash. What they hadn't expected Claude to do was resist them, but he did. As one of the men stayed in the car as a lookout, the other went into Claude's house and beat him unmercifully with the brass knuckles.

Uncle Claude owned a pistol that just happened to be on the kitchen table. When Uncle Claude somehow managed to stand up, even after the beating, and threaten to get his gun, the robber ran to the kitchen first and got the gun. Uncle Claude was shot twice; the first shot hit him in the neck and severed his jugular vein. The second shot, at close range, in the back of his head shattered his brain.

In his confession to the police, the shooter said, "I ran from the house, jumped in the car," and told his accomplice, "I just killed a man." His friend looked at him in disbelief and said, "No you didn't."

"Didn't you hear the shots?"

"Yes, but I didn't want to believe it."

The shooter and his accomplice realized pretty quickly that they had moved from small time hoodlums to big time felons. They fled the scene, threw the pistol and the brass knuckles in a creek some miles away, and hid Uncle Claude's wallet in a tree. All together, they got $350 from Uncle Claude. "I could hardly spend it," said the murderer in his confession, "but I wanted to get rid of it, so I bought some guitar strings, concert tickets, and drugs."

It wasn't long before the accomplice confessed to the police. Both he and the shooter were arrested, and both confessed. The pistol and the brass knuckles were recovered from the creek to be used as evidence in the trial. Because of their confessions and the evidence against them, they both decided to seek a plea bargain. The district attorney worked out a deal where the accomplice pled guilty to armed robbery and accessory to second-degree murder and the shooter pled guilty to armed robbery and second-degree murder. The shooter was sentenced to life in prison.

My aunt had come home and found her husband, dead in a pool of blood. My Uncle Claude was not the only victim of the crime. His wife, his children and grandchildren, the extended family, and every member of the small community around Uncle Claude's house were victims, too. Crimes of violence have repercussions which last for generations. One of the really sad realities that became very apparent to me was that the victims and extended families of victims of crime had no rights.

The criminals were guaranteed all kinds of rights – the right to a speedy trial, the right to adequate legal council (usually two attorneys paid for by the taxpayers), the right to remain silent, the right to know in advance what all of the legal proceedings would be and when they would be held, the right to a jury trial and to be tried by a jury of their peers, the right to know all of the evidence against them, and the right to know, in advance, what the prosecutor's theory of the case is and how it would be tried. The victims and the victim's families had none of these rights.

In Uncle Claude's case, the prosecutor was nice enough to let my aunt know that the defendants were probably going to plead guilty. She was, quite frankly, willing to put it all behind her and just move on, which is a typical coping mechanism for victims. The problem is, it's almost impossible to put a violent crime behind you. The prosecuting attorney was not required to inform the victim's family of anything. It was clear to me that the victims of crime and their families were often victimized over and over again by the process.

Uncle Claude's killer was sentenced to life in prison. He is no longer in prison. Two years ago, the family received notice that he was about to be paroled. The family had not received notice that he was even up for parole. Like most families, we thought that life in prison meant life in prison.

The first time I ran for the legislature, I made crime prevention a major campaign issue. While I was campaigning, a person brought me a piece of yellow police "crime scene" tape.

"When you come home and find this tape all around your house, it's too late for crime prevention," he said. "Take this tape to remind you that there are a lot of victims of crime out there."

That piece of yellow tape hung on the wall of my office in the legislature. I'm sure that my political opponents thought that my office was, indeed, a crime scene. But the tape was there to remind me. Victim's rights were to become one of the most important issues and accomplishments of my tenure in the House.

Crime is, unfortunately, always with us. Every society has criminals. But the society should not add a crime to a crime by failing to support those who are victims of criminals.

Chapter 12

NC House District 40

***"I live for those who love me, for those who know me true;
For the heaven that smiles above me, and awaits my spirit too;
For the cause that lacks assistance, for the
wrong that needs resistance,
For the future in the distance, for the good that I can do."***

—G. L. BANKS IN *MY AIM*

I was first elected to the North Carolina House of Representatives as a part of the Republican sweep of 1994. The victory gave the Republicans their first majority in the House since Reconstruction. Sixty-one members are required for a majority in the House, and the Republicans had a working majority of 68.

The Republican Party had also swept to victory in the national election. Riding on the "Contract with America," the Congress had large Republican majorities in both the House and Senate. The Congress moved quickly to enact the legislation called for in the contract. On the national level things could not have been better for Republicans.

But things were different in North Carolina. Even though the Republicans held the majority in the House, the Senate was still controlled by the Democrats. The Democrats could block the initiatives of the House, and the Republicans could block the initiatives of the Senate. Gridlock was the order of the day.

But an even greater problem than gridlock faced the Republicans – we couldn't come together on an agenda. Republicans said that they were for commonsense government. The problem is that common sense isn't very common, especially in politics, and the Republican legislators never came to a consensus.

As a freshman legislator, I was at a loss. I didn't understand the system. I didn't really know what I wanted to accomplish and I wasn't sure how to get anything accomplished. The first few weeks were eye opening. I was trying to figure out how the process worked. The general wisdom is that a legislator spends his first term discovering where the restrooms are, his second term learning who is stopping his initiatives, and his third term learning how to get back at those who were stopping him and pass his introduced legislation. It wasn't quite that bad, but almost.

Even though I wasn't quite sure how the process worked, I did know that I had been elected to represent the people of my district. I knew that if I had good constituent service I would be a good legislator. For me, good constituent service meant listening to the concerns of the people of my district and allowing the voters to actually have input into the proposed laws. I knew that, ultimately, I would actually have to make a decision on each issue and cast a vote, but I wanted to have as much input from the voters of my district as I could get.

I also learned very quickly that one person, working alone, could never accomplish anything. Mavericks might be able to kick up a ruckus to stop something from happening. Sometimes, that's a good thing. Voters often sent us the message, "Don't do anything to us!" But the ultimate purpose of the legislature is to actually do things to make the government of North Carolina work for the people. Obstructionism needs to give way to commonsense solutions to solve real problems.

Politics, whether we like it or not, is involved in every aspect of our lives. The quality of the water we drink, the food we eat, and the air we breathe are determined by politics. The schools our children attend, the jobs that are available to our citizens, and the roads we drive on to get to them are all influenced by politics. It is only through politics that the government can provide a system of justice and fair play for its citizens.

It was in the realm of justice that I found my first true niche – my first political crusade. When I moved into my office in the legislative building, I hung that piece of police "crime scene" tape my constituent had given me on the wall to remind me of the need to bring down the crime rate in North Carolina. I hadn't really thought much about helping the victims of crime, but my "crime scene" tape drew the attention of the North Carolina Victims Assistance Network (NCVAN). For more than ten years prior to my coming to the legislature, this group of concerned citizens had been pushing for a Victims Rights Amendment to the North Carolina Constitution.

As I talked with members of NCVAN, it dawned on me that the state was often guilty of perpetrating a series of crimes against the victims of crime.

- The victims of crime had no right to be informed of the court proceedings against the accused or even to be present at the proceedings.
- Victims had no right to be heard at the sentencing if the accused had been convicted.
- Victims had no right of restitution.
- Victims had no right to be present at parole hearings or to address the parole board.
- Victims of crime had limited access to the prosecutors.
- The victims were not even informed if the accused was released on parole, or escaped incarceration.

Having been a victim of crime (indirectly) when my uncle was murdered, I had experienced some of the frustration that those more closely connected with the crimes of murder and rape had also experienced. But as I listened to the members of NCVAN, I realized more fully the deep hurt and pain that crime brings into the lives of victims.

I quickly joined in the fight for the constitutional amendment. It takes three-fifths of the members of both houses of the legislature to recommend an amendment to the people, and a majority of all voters must approve before it becomes a part of the constitution. I was just one small voice in the process and, in 1995, the voters of North Carolina overwhelmingly approved a "Rights of Victims of Crime" Amendment to be added to Article 1 – The Declaration of Rights. There was one big problem. The amendment left it to the general assembly to pass all of the legislation required to implement the constitutional rights of crime victims.

Some of the members of NCVAN asked me to spearhead the legislation. The process was my true baptism into politics. I was stunned by the opposition. The voters had overwhelmingly approved the amendment and instructed the assembly to act, but the opponents had several arguments against implementation:

- Victims were not getting equal rights; they were getting special rights.
- Gays and lesbians wanted to be included as victims.
- Democrats didn't want the Republican-controlled House to get credit for legislation that would implement the amendment.
- Republicans didn't want the Democratic-controlled Senate to get credit.

- If the legislation passed, it was going to cost big bucks to implement. Neither party wanted a tax increase, but neither party was willing to take the money from existing programs.

It took two years (two years!), to pass the legislation. But once the dam broke, a literal flood of legislation followed. From 1996 through 2004, the general assembly passed fourteen major bills related to crime victims. The bills had many positive effects:

- To increase the compensation available to crime victims to cover the costs of burial.
- To require the governor to provide notice to victims of any sentence commutation.
- To require notification of victims of a defendant's release.
- To give victims the right to offer evidence of the crime's impact on their lives.
- To notify the victim within twenty-four hours if the defendant should escape custody.
- To prohibit death row inmates from contacting victims' family members without the prior consent of the victims.
- To provide that the defendant be incarcerated in an out-of-county facility for the safety of the victim or immediate family.
- To provide the right for two members of the crime victim's family to be present when the offender is executed if they desire to do so for closure.
- To require that the sentence "life in prison without the possibility of parole" actually mean life without parole. Prior to the implementation of this act, judges in North

Carolina were required *by law* to answer "yes" if juries asked the question, "Does life in prison without parole really mean life in prison?" even though life in prison really meant a twenty-five year sentence.

- To provide that felons not profit from their crimes.

Working on each of these pieces of legislation was one of the great privileges of my time in the assembly. This letter, which I received in 2001, is an example of the response of the public (I have edited it slightly by omitting the names).

> *Rick,*
>
> *I cannot express on paper or words the help, time, caring, and kindness you have shown through our times of troubles and worrying over this case.*
>
> *I am so grateful that God made a person like you; you are a kind, gentle person. If we had more leaders like you, what a better world this would be to live in. In my book, you are a very outstanding person in our community.*
>
> *May God bless you and your family.*
>
> *Thank you so very, very, much for your time and concern.*

Letters like that tend to make politics worth it all.

The system is not yet perfect. Several years ago, I received a notification from the parole board that the murderer of my uncle was coming up for parole. The parole hearing was scheduled for October 27th and the letter was postmarked October 29th. Fortunately, the hearing had actually been postponed, and my family was able to participate in the hearing when it was held.

As long as there are criminals, there will be victims. The state should do everything in its power to enact necessary laws and ensure that the judicial and executive branches administer the laws enacted to ease the hurt of victims and correct the injustices which criminals bring.

Chapter 13

Witness an Execution

"The administration of justice is the firmest pillar of government."
—GEORGE WASHINGTON

Each time a person is executed by the State of North Carolina, a representative of the state must be present as an official witness. In my first term in the general assembly, I was asked by a member of the governor's staff to represent the state at the execution of a convicted murderer.

I'm not exactly sure why I was asked. I had taken two strong stands –victim's rights and strident support for the death penalty – early in my legislative days. I may have been asked to witness the execution because the governor's staff was trying to soften my views. Or, I may have been asked because I was such a hardliner that being the witness wouldn't bother me.

After a couple days of thinking about it, I told the staffer that I would be the witness. I was given credentials, a special parking pass to Central Prison, and the phone number that would connect me directly to the warden. The date was set, but there are often delays, usually stays sought by the convict's lawyers or death penalty opponents and offered by sympathetic judges. I was instructed to call the phone number about an hour before I was scheduled to arrive to make sure that the execution was proceeding.

Executions in North Carolina are scheduled at 2:00 a.m. The witnesses, the prison staff who are participating, and the executioners are required to be at the prison four hours early. At 9:00 p.m., I called the warden's number and he informed me that all appeals had been heard and that the execution was proceeding. I was instructed to be at the prison at 10.

The drive from my home in North Raleigh to Central Prison seemed unusually long. I certainly wasn't looking forward to the night's events. When I pulled onto the prison grounds, I was met by a crowd of death penalty opponents holding a candlelight vigil. These people were certainly strong believers. They would stand and burn candles for up to five hours as a silent protest against the State of North Carolina murdering a man by execution.

Because I had credentials and a parking pass, I was directed to a place in the inner sanctum of the prison and met by the warden. As we walked from the parking lot to the death row area, he explained the process. The felon had already had his final meal. He would be given about an hour to visit with his family and another hour to visit with his clergyman (or prison chaplain). He would also be offered a snack and be given the opportunity to make a final statement for the record. About two hours before the execution, he would be given a shot to calm him down. In the last hour, the final preparations would begin.

When I arrived on death row, I was introduced to the inmate. He was sitting at a small round table in the common area. The warden told him that I was one of the official witnesses.

"Is there a large vigil outside?" he asked.

"Yes," I replied.

"Are you a reporter?" he asked.

"No," I replied. Those were to be the only words we spoke to each other.

There are not many words that can describe death row and the death chamber – cold, eerie, sterile – there was a strange combination of silence punctuated with noise. Each time one of the doors to death row opened or closed, a loud clanging penetrated every core of my being. A TV, with absolutely awful reception, was on, but no one was paying any attention to it. I am sure that it was on just to provide noise.

I would have preferred total silence, but I understood the need for some noise. I could almost see the silence, like a dark cloud blotting out the sun.

I was surprised at how many people were there. There were at least eight guards. One of them controlled the doors. One was taking notes, recording everything that happened for some kind of official record. The other six seemed to be unnecessary, but their duty was to become obvious later. There was a nurse and a doctor; the prison chaplain, the warden, and myself. I was given a tour of the death chamber. It's a small, oddly shaped room with a drape jutting out into the middle of it. I saw that the witness area was on one side of the partition – behind a glass wall there were sixteen chairs. On the other side of the partition, hidden from the witnesses, was where I would stand with the doctor and warden. On a table were the machines that would monitor the breathing and heart rate.

About 11:00, the prisoner was asked if he wanted a snack. He said that he wanted a Coke and a cinnamon bun. I don't know if this had been prearranged, but a Coke and cinnamon bun appeared in just moments. The prisoner sat in his cell, eating his snack.

I thought of my Uncle Claude. His murderer had not given him the opportunity to enjoy a last meal, or a last snack.

The chaplain spent the next hour with him. Scripture was read. Prayers were said. Part of the time, they just sat in silence. At the end of the chaplain's time, he and the inmate said the "Lord's Prayer" together and the chaplain left. The nurse and a guard entered, led him to his cell and a shot was given that was to make the condemned man groggy. It wasn't long before he stopped moving around in his cell and lay down on his bed.

About one o'clock, the six guards entered his cell with a gurney. They placed him on the stretcher, strapped him to it, made him form his hands into fists and then completely covered each fist with tape. He didn't resist, but he didn't exactly cooperate either. About one-thirty, the doctor began the process of putting in the IV port through which the lethal injection would enter his body.

At about 1:50, the doctor indicated that all was ready. The warden went up to the convict and read to him the statement about his guilt and the just punishment which the state was about to administer. The condemned was given the opportunity to make a final statement, but he simply shook his head, no.

"May God have mercy on your soul." The words really are spoken. I don't want to condemn a man or woman to eternal damnation (although some family members of the victim might). I understand that the death penalty is about justice, not revenge.

The gurney was rolled into the execution chamber. The doctor and I were in a small room the size of a closet with a glass window. There was complete silence. Everything had already been said. We simply stood there and watched the monitors. After a few minutes, they stopped blinking. A man was dead.

As we left the death chamber, I noticed that nearly everyone present, the guards, the doctor, the chaplain, were crying or nearly crying. They weren't sobbing, but tears were rolling down their cheeks or welling up in their eyes. The awful finality of what they were called to do was overwhelming.

I didn't shed a tear. I was thinking of my Uncle Claude.

As I was escorted back to the exit door by one of the guards, I saw the hearse, waiting to pick up the body. I thought of my Uncle Claude lying in a pool of blood.

When I drove out of the prison, the candlelight vigil was still going strong. I supposed those people would stay and keep their candles burning in the darkness until the hearse pulled away.

As I was driving home, the silence in the car suddenly became too much. I turned on the radio for some noise. "The State of North Carolina has just executed…" the announcer said. That wasn't the noise I wanted to hear. I turned the radio off.

As I drove home in the overpowering silence, I felt dirty. I knew that justice had been done, but I had personally discovered that justice, like politics, is sometimes a dirty business.

I walked in the house and went straight to the shower. It may have been the longest shower I have ever taken.

I climbed into bed beside Sherry. In her sleep, she rolled over and put her arm around me. Only her breathing broke the silence. It was one of the most beautiful sounds that I have ever heard.

Fighting a Moratorium

I understand that there are significant arguments against the death penalty, and strong support for the penalty. I, of course, am a supporter of the ultimate penalty. I believe that the death penalty is

- Biblical
- Just and fair
- A great deterrent
- The best source of closure for victims' families

I understand that the opponents of the death penalty have serious, well-considered arguments as well. They believe that the death penalty is

- Unbiblical
- Unjust and unfair
- No deterrent to crime
- Unfairly applied
- A form of vengeance
- Legalized murder by the state
- The result of prosecutorial misconduct, or the inadequacy of lawyers representing murder defendants

In 2003, a moratorium on the death penalty was proposed in the General Assembly. Sponsored by liberal Democrats, it would have been the first moratorium in the nation sponsored by a legislature. Two states, Illinois and Maryland, had had moratoriums proclaimed by their governors.

The purpose of the moratorium was, according to its sponsors, the opportunity to study all of the various issues related to the death penalty. If the moratorium passed, a fifteen member commission would be established and given two to three years to study the issues while all executions would be halted. If passed, the commission would have had five members appointed by the Senate leader, five members appointed by the speaker of the house, and five appointed by the governor.

As a strong advocate for victim's rights and for the death penalty, I was tabbed by the Republicans in the House (with the silent support of some conservative Democrats) to lead the opposition to the moratorium. The battle was waged in the House. The Senate had enough votes to pass the moratorium, even though the governor was opposed and polls showed that the majority of the people of North Carolina were also opposed.

The argument for the moratorium gained strength when two high profile murder convictions were tossed out by the courts. One of the death-row inmates had his conviction overturned because prosecutors or police withheld evidence that might have freed him, and in the second, DNA evidence surfaced which proved the inmate's innocence.

"If even one innocent man or woman is executed," the supporters of the moratorium argued, "it would be a tragedy which could never be forgiven." The supporters argued that it would be "better to let 1000 guilty men go free than to execute one innocent one."

Even though their arguments were valid, there were equally valid counter-arguments. The very fact that two innocent men were set free by the courts proved to me and the opponents of the moratorium that North Carolina's judicial system was working. The moratorium supporters never actually had enough votes to pass the bill in the House, but the numbers were very close.

There was intensive lobbying on both sides. It was one of those issues where party lines were not as distinct as usual. Though the majority of Republicans opposed the bill and the majority of Democrats supported it, there was more than the usual number of defections on both sides. The most effective lobbying against the moratorium came from the North Carolina Victims Assistance Network. At that time, there were 202 people on death row in North Carolina. Each of the 202 persons had a unique story to tell, but so did their victims' families. The most powerful form of lobbying came, not from lobbyists or organized groups, but from just one victim sharing his or her deep pain with a legislator. NCVAN organized victims who would come to Raleigh or call to speak directly to their own representative. As the members of the

House heard and felt the pain, saw the deep (and often) unending grief of the victims, they were deeply moved. The House never had enough votes to pass the moratorium.

As strong as the arguments against the death penalty are, the cause of justice demands that it be kept in place. Absolutely no one wants to execute an innocent person! With new technology, especially DNA evidence, it is becoming less and less likely that an innocent person will be convicted and sentenced to death.

It is clear to me that the moratorium, if passed, was just the first step in eliminating the death penalty in North Carolina altogether. Many groups continue to work to accomplish that goal. But the death penalty is always a major issue back home. When legislators have to go home to campaign, they have to face their voters, and in the vast majority of districts in our state, the people are pro death penalty.

A day or two before the bill was to be brought to the floor for final debate and a vote, I made a statement which looked much worse in print than it was meant to be: "They don't have the votes. They don't need to bring it up. They might as well take it off the calendar and forget it." I can't remember anything that I said in twelve years in the assembly, which made my opponents angrier. They believed that I was thumbing my nose at them or that I was trying to cut off debate on a critical issue.

I actually welcome the debate. And I welcome a commission to study the death penalty, and all of the concerns expressed by the opposition. What I don't welcome is a moratorium which would halt executions. If only one innocent life is saved because of the deterrent of the death penalty; if only one family gets closure; if justice is served, then our system has fulfilled its purpose.

Let the debate continue!

Chapter 14

Smells Like $$ to Some, Stink to Others

"A statesman is a successful politician who is dead."
—SENATOR HENRY CABOT LODGE

I began this book by announcing that "pigs don't know pigs stink." But humans surely do know it. It is such a shame that an animal that tastes so good produces so much waste – the fancy term is effluence – that smells like...well, you know what it smells like.

North Carolina is the second largest hog producing state in the nation, behind only Iowa. On any given day there are about 10 million hogs being raised on about 3,600 farms in North Carolina, mostly in the southeastern counties.

Pork production is big business! There are about 46,000 full-time, well-paid jobs in the hog industry in North Carolina. Most of the pork products come from large corporate farms.

There are three major problems with the hog industry, all related to the fact that the average hog produces about four times more waste everyday than the average human: the odor, the pollution of the ground water and streams, and the effects of uncontrolled spraying of the effluence. Hog waste is collected in large, specially dug lagoons. The waste is treated each day and eventually forms a liquid that is a great, nitrogen-rich fertilizer if applied at the right time and in the proper manner.

Prior to me serving in office, the industry sponsored a bill that passed the legislature that exempted all hog farms from any local zoning ordinances. It was a major boon to the industry and many farmers, who were seeing the price of tobacco fall, turned to large hog operations as their major source of income. In 1996, the legislature reversed itself and placed a two-year moratorium on the construction of new or expansion of existing corporate hog farms.

Rumor was the industry planned to build a hog production facility in Moore County. Moore County is home to one of the nation's oldest and most popular golfing resorts, Pinehurst. The representative who represented the county introduced a local bill that would have prohibited this construction or the construction of any hog production facility in Moore County. It quickly became clear that this local bill should become a state bill, and both the House and the Senate moved to consider the extension of the moratorium statewide.

The battle lines were drawn. In one corner was the hog industry, with its deep pockets and all of the jobs, which it represents. In the other corner were the environmental lobbyists with their passion for clean water and air. In another corner was the tourist industry, determined to stop anything which would negatively affect tourism in North Carolina. In yet another corner were the row crop farmers, small farmers who happened to be located next door to corporate hog operations and were those most likely to bear the negative consequences of spills or over spray. In addition to all of these sides was the fact that the majority of the large hog operations were located in the economically poorest counties, primarily among African American, Native American and Hispanic populations.

As co-chair of the House Environment Committee (because I was appointed to be the Environmental Review Commission Chairman, I was effectively the chair), I became the eye in the center of the storm. I was lobbied hard from all sides. One night at a dinner with members of the Farm Bureau, I happened to sit at a table with farmers who didn't own hogs but did live close enough to the hog operations that they were negatively affected. If the hog farmers sprayed the effluent on windy days, the wind would carry the waste onto their property – their homes, cars, children's toys, and farm equipment – all covered with a sticky, smelly mess one of them told me. A second problem was that if the effluent happened to be sprayed on a day that it also rained, the run-off would pollute the area water systems. And the flies were everywhere!

Eye of the Storm

A few days later, I was offered a trip by small plane down the Neuse River to see for myself the effect that over spraying of fields and spills from the lagoons (or intentional discharges) were having on the environment. The trip was being offered by the River Keepers, an environmental group. At first, I was reluctant to go, because I knew that I would get a pretty one-sided view of things. I initially turned down the River Keepers, but because of the serious nature of the issue, I later accepted their offer.

We flew from Knightdale to New Bern along the Neuse River. I was stunned that I could actually see, from the air, the negative effects. The grounds around lagoons where there had been discharges and the streams and creeks nearby were brown with death. Further down the streams and into the river itself there were patches of a deep green algae growing in running water, the result of too much nitrogen in the water. It was also clear to me, from the air, that many of the lagoons, which were specially built to hold and treat the waste were completely full, were located too close to existing streams and rivers, and were a disaster waiting to happen. [Later that year, the North Carolina Division of

Water Quality found that 42% of the lagoons had discharges that year and that 25% of these spills ran directly into surface waters.]

At a later time, I was also given a tour of a hog operation. It really was a treat. It is simply amazing that pork production is such a technologically advanced industry. I was stunned at the size of the houses, the number of hogs, the feeding operations, and the waste management controls. Raising hogs is big business, and big business always wants to run effectively and profitably. Hog farmers may be businessmen, but they are also farmers and they know that, ultimately, their livelihoods come from the land. So they, too, are environmentalists. They want what is best for the land, but they also wanted to grow their businesses and the proposed moratorium would not allow them to do so.

Being in the eye of the storm was a fascinating place to be. Every side had legitimate concerns. Every side had legitimate arguments. As co-chair of the committee, I was determined that there was to be open and fair debate. I scheduled committee meetings and invited representatives from all sides to express their views.

I thought that public debate and conversation was a good thing. I thought that I was being a good statesman. The environmentalists, the tourist industry, the row crop farmers, some members of the Black Caucus, and the press thought it was terrible! They were all convinced that I was delaying any vote so that the bill would die in committee, or that I was filibustering until the pork producers could muster enough support to stop the moratorium. I was actually in favor of the moratorium, but I wanted there to be a more extensive law that would require stronger environmental controls, and, if met, would allow the industry to actually expand.

Saved by the Sergeant-of-Arms

At one of the committee meetings, the anti-swine activists (swine sounds so much worse than hogs or pork, doesn't it?) were furious that I did not bring the bill to a vote. Nearly one hundred very loud and very angry activists surrounded me, shouting questions or epithets (which sounded a lot like hog waste smells) and tried to literally back me into a corner of the meeting room. They were so angry, that the General Assembly's sergeant-at-arms had to come to my rescue. I literally had to be saved from an angry mob inside the legislative office building. The Raleigh *News and Observer* sided with the mob; they accused me of obfuscation, obstructionism, and basic dirty dealing, when all I really wanted was a law that addressed everyone's concerns. I held on long enough in committee, that the hog industry finally came to realize that I wasn't in their pocket as the N&O was implying.

I knew that there were plenty of votes in the committee and the assembly to overwhelmingly pass the moratorium. But I also knew that if I could get the many sides to actually talk to one another that some good would come from it. The environmentalists were accusing the hog industry of polluting the streams and rivers while the hog industry was accusing the row farmers of causing the pollution through overuse of pesticides and fertilizers. The fact was that no one really knew for sure who was at fault, but that there were tests that the State Division of Water Quality could run to determine the actual source. The more we talked, the more it became apparent to all concerned that everybody was pointing fingers, but nobody was actually seeking solutions. The breakthrough had come!

The end result was that the Hog Bill moratorium passed the legislature with ease and has easily been re-passed each time it has arisen.

Another result was that the hog industry, itself, rose to the occasion and strengthened the lagoon system. Except for the horrific flooding which occurred as a result of Hurricane Floyd, the devastation no one could have foreseen, the number of spills has been dramatically decreased, over spraying has been self-regulated, and the industry is spending hundreds of thousands of dollars a year in research to eliminate the odor pollution.

Although it takes a majority of the legislature to pass any bill, this issue is a very good example of how one person can make a difference. I took the heat from the press, from the lobbyists, from the activists, from the concerned voters in my district, and stood my ground. The industry was growing so fast, the environmental effects were so great, and the potential harm was so intense that something had to be done!

Sometimes, the winds of change blow in softly. Sometimes they are a hurricane.

Chapter 15

Attacking Failing Schools

"He who opens a school door, closes a prison."
—VICTOR HUGO

The right for the citizens of North Carolina to be educated in public schools is guaranteed in our state's constitution. The problem is that the state cannot guarantee a quality education. Public schools in North Carolina, and every other state in the union, carry a larger percentage of the state and local budgets than any other item. We continue to pour more and more money into the public schools even though up to half of the schools fail to educate their students!

In the 2005-2006 school year, North Carolina spent $7,000 per pupil on public education, not including the cost of school buildings, which is funded through bonds. With an average class size of 28 students in the elementary schools, that means that the state, local, and federal tax payers invested $196,000 per classroom per year to teach our kids. The average teacher salary in North Carolina in 2006 was $36,500. Where in the world is the extra $153,500 going? And is the state getting its money's worth?

The public education debate has many aspects. There are those who are convinced that the public schools in the state (and throughout the nation) are a complete failure, that the system we have now should be scrapped, and that continuing to uphold the present system is an utter waste of taxpayer's dollars. There are others who point to the fact that many of our high school graduates go on to perform at an exceptional level in colleges and universities and that the public schools should be given credit for preparing them.

Part of the great problem which faces the public schools in North Carolina is that the vast majority of private schools exceed the public schools in their ability to educate their students, and they do it with far less expense per student. There is no doubt that the majority of private schools in the state were founded as a direct result of the integration of the public schools in the 1960's and 70's. Even though they were often Christian schools, they didn't act Christian when it came to race relations. Private schools were seen, rightly or wrongly, as racist institutions, and though they did a good job of educating their students in the basics, they did an extremely poor job of preparing their students to live in a racially diverse society.

School Vouchers

From the 60's through the 90's, parents who were spending their hard-earned money on tuition for private schools and were also being taxed for funding public schools sought relief from the state. They argued that they were entitled to help from the state in the education of their children. Each session of the legislature, these parents would appeal to their representatives to institute a voucher system, whereby parents who paid for their children to receive a private education would receive a voucher from the state equal to the amount of money that the state spent on each student for public education. That "vouchered" money could then be used by the taxpayer to help pay the tuition for his child's private school.

The democratically controlled assembly would never consider the voucher idea. The idea was an anathema to the North Carolina Association of Educators (NCAE), the teachers union which represents the public school teachers, and one of the largest contributors to the Democratic Party and its candidates. The NCAE's most prevalent argument against the vouchers was that it would be robbing the public schools of money.

Look Out for Charter Schools

When the Republican Party took control of the House in 1994, the political landscape of the state shifted dramatically. For the Republicans, the voucher system was a major emphasis, though the name was changed to tuition tax credits. The Democrats still controlled the Senate, so there was no way that the proposal would ever be passed, but at least a public debate could be held.

In 1996, the House included $30 million in the state budget to fund Tuition Tax Credits. The NCAE and the Democrats were furious! To say that there was tremendous controversy would be to put it mildly. The NCAE argued that the proposal would take public money from the schools and turn it over to private industry. The fact that the majority of the private schools were all-white simply added to the controversy. The Republicans countered with the argument that the public schools were failing in their mandate to educate the children. The Republicans rightly asked the question, "Why should the state continue to fully fund a failing system?"

The debate was intense, but it opened the way for a compromise – charter schools. Charter schools are open to all people, receive public money equal to the per student expenditure that the state is spending on other public schools, and don't charge tuition. The charter schools are run by private boards instead of locally elected school boards, and administrators don't have to follow all of the regulations imposed on traditional public schools. Charter schools must have a charter which is approved by the State Board of Education.

Making Education History

Since I served as vice-chairman of the Education Committee when the Charter School legislation was introduced, I was privileged to be a part of this history-making law. I was also picked to be a member of the conference committee to work out the differences between the House and Senate versions of the bill. The bill that the House passed was more far-reaching than the Senate version – it included an unlimited number of charter schools in the state and a specific requirement that all of the public colleges and universities and community colleges in the state be encouraged to start charter schools as a feeder program for their institutions. The House bill also allowed successful charter schools to franchise themselves. All of these provisions had to be dropped in the conference; it was clear that we had to get what we could from the Senate and hope that the charter schools would be so successful that they would be more readily supported in the future. The bill that was ultimately approved included a cap of no more than 100 schools in the state with no more than five per school district. (The five per district limit has since been waived. Wake County has 19 of the 99 charter schools currently in operation in the state).

The ultimate purpose of the Charter School Legislation was to improve the public education system of North Carolina. Supporters of the law believed (and still believe) that competition would be a good thing for the public schools. In the ten years that the charter schools have been operating in the state, the debate about their effectiveness has continued.

The North Carolina Center for Public Policy Research has concluded that the charter schools "have not done as well as traditional public schools," and that "53 percent of them were finishing in the bottom three categories on academic performance under the state ABC accountability testing system."

Other reports found the opposite to be the case. The John Locke Society reported that "North Carolina's Charter Schools have low average school and class sizes, innovative curriculum and instructional approaches, few disciplinary problems, and student performance that is comparable to the public schools."

One of the arguments against the charter school concept was that it would encourage "white flight" from the public schools. The opposite has been true. The black community has embraced charter schools as a way of addressing the chronic problem of underachieving public schools. Thirty-nine of 99 charter schools in the state have a black student population of 50% or more and fourteen of the schools have a black student population of 95%. North Carolina's population is approximately 22% black. Charter school supporters see the racial disparity as a good thing. The North Carolina Office of Charter Schools in a recent newsletter said that the schools "reflect the special population that each school seeks to serve," and some schools "have focused their attention on helping black students."

Shut Them Down

The fact is that students in charter schools in North Carolina have academic performances which meet or exceed the performance of students in the traditional public schools. This is especially significant since the charter schools in the state tend to be schools which focus on students who are academically challenged or have failed to perform up to grade level in the traditional schools.

The charter school system isn't perfect. Some charter schools have failed, and when they have failed, they have been shut down. But almost half of all of the public schools in the state have a chronic failure rate, and, yet, continue to be fully funded by the taxpayers.

The great need for the charter school system is for the state to allow an unlimited number of charter schools. There is, of course, tremendous opposition to such a bold move. Since the law was enacted, the legislators of each session of the assembly have considered proposals to eliminate the cap of 100 altogether or to expand the cap. Each year, these proposals have failed. The NCAE and the North Carolina Center for Public Policy Research have been the strongest opponents. In their latest report (July 2007), the NCPPR director said, "The charter schools experiment has been a failure. Don't expand the experiment before you've got something that works."

To label the charter school experiment a failure is to ignore the facts. To point to a few charter schools that have failed and condemn the whole process in disingenuous. Such a position ignores the great complexity of what the charter school movement is hoping to accomplish, what great success there has been, and the potential for dramatic change in the public education system in North Carolina.

As a member of the General Assembly who helped to get the legislation passed, I believed that it was important for me to put my money where my mouth is and do all that I could to establish a charter school in my House district. The next chapter of the book is about one of my greatest personal success stories – Franklin Academy.

Chapter 16

School of Excellence

"The quality of a person's life is in direct proportion to their commitment to excellence."

—VINCE LOMBARDI

Nationwide, there are about 85,000 public schools with about 52,000,000 students and about 2,650,000 teachers. On all levels (local, county, state, and federal) the government spent about $360 billion dollars on public schools in 2006.

In spite of the incredible expenditure of funds, there are alarming facts about our public schools:

- 30% of all ninth graders will fail to graduate in four years. Less that 50% of ninth graders in urban schools will graduate in four years.
- 14% of all students will drop out completely. The rate is 15% for black children, 36% for Hispanic children, and 30% for children from low-income families.
- American students spend less than half of their school day, or about three hours, on core academic studies. Although U.S. students spend more time in school than students of most other industrialized countries (about 1,000 hours a year) more than half of their time is taken up by non-academic pursuits such as driver's education and counseling.

- In the last 30 years, the national average SAT score has decreased by 36%.
- Only 37% of twelfth graders reach a proficient level of reading. (That means that 63% of the recent high school graduates in America would have trouble reading this book!)
- Only 25% of twelfth graders are proficient in math. Half of all twelfth graders cannot solve problems which include fractions, decimals or percents or that draw on elementary concepts of geometry or algebra.
- Two-thirds of recent high school graduates failed to identify in which century the Civil War was fought; 60% could not identify the purpose of the Emancipation Proclamation, and only one-third knew the significance of the Supreme Court ruling on Brown v. Board of Education.

All of these disturbing statistics came from the Center for Education Reform in Washington, D.C. They are a clear indication that the public school system in America is failing! [If you are interested in knowing more, read *The School Reform Handbook* by Jeanne Allen, president of the center.]

All of these statistics are a mandate for reform! I am not, as some right-wingers are, an advocate for doing away with public education. I know that the public schools will be with us, but dramatic change is needed. I believe that competition is the key to reform – that good schools will attract good students and that the competition will cause poor schools to get better.

Some of the most effective public schools in the country are charter schools. I was privileged to be a part of starting one of the best, Franklin Academy Charter School. When I was serving on the House

Education Committee and working to establish the charter school program in North Carolina, I became acquainted with Bob Luddy, a successful businessman from Raleigh who has a passion for improving the public schools. Bob Luddy was a strong advocate for charter schools, worked tirelessly to help get the charter school legislation passed, and became the founder of Franklin Academy.

Franklin Academy is a "state of the art" charter school.

Bob Luddy asked me to serve on the board of the new school. Our first task was to decide on the kind of school that we wanted, and to develop a charter which would reflect our goals. One of the great challenges facing charter schools is that their charters have to be approved by the State Department of Public Instruction. That means, of course, that every "t" has to be crossed and every "i" dotted. The charter must include a mission statement, graduation requirements, and a set of specific goals that can be measured by the state.

As it turned out, putting together our charter and getting it approved by the state were the easiest things we did. It was putting together a school that proved to be really difficult. We had to find a location, hire a staff, find all of the necessary equipment (desks, tables, chairs, books, computers – the list goes on and on) and recruit the students. Finding the location proved to be the most challenging task.

We first looked at an abandoned hospital in Wake Forest. The hospital had been a part of the Wake County health system and the county owned the building. Even though the building was not in use and was falling into disrepair, it was in a great location. We were willing to invest the money that was necessary to upgrade the building and to lease it from the county, but the county was unwilling to even consider a lease.

We then looked at an abandoned school, the DuBois School, also in Wake Forest. The DuBois School had been the black school in Wake Forest before integration. The nine buildings which comprised the school were in terrible condition. For nineteen years, the buildings had sat unused and uncared for. All of the roofs had leaks and needed replacement. All of the heating and air conditioning systems were inadequate, and much of the electrical systems needed updating. The old school did not have as good a location as the hospital, but it had great potential.

A group of DuBois School alumni had been trying for years to raise the funds to purchase the property from the county. They dreamed of starting a community outreach center. The Franklin Academy board entered into an agreement with the alumni association to give the association two of the nine buildings, the gymnasium and the Culler Building, the newest and largest building on campus for the use of the community center and Franklin Academy would use the remaining campus.

The school board had been asking $390,000 for the property which included seventeen acres, but it had sold several other abandoned properties to other groups for much less (on average about

10% of their asking price). We went to the school board and offered $30,000, promising to upgrade all of the facilities and promising to donate two of the buildings to the alumni association. Since a charter school is a public school, it made sense that the purchase price be much less. The county would be getting a new public school after all. If the school board turned down the deal, Luddy promised to purchase the entire property for the $390,000 asking price and to donate money to the alumni association to help renovate the two buildings which would comprise the community center. We even had a press conference on the site to celebrate the rebirth of DuBois School.

It was then that politics truly came into play. Members of the alumni association began to ask for more and more. Members of the county commissioners were upset that they had been "excluded" from the negotiations. Members of the school board, suspicious of charter schools, suddenly had future plans for a property that had been abandoned since 1989. The town of Wake Forest insisted that sidewalks be built from the main road to the school property (about four blocks) which would require moving all of the utility poles. Eventually, the entire deal fell apart, and Franklin Academy was homeless.

The only option that remained was to *build* a school. We purchased land outside of Wake Forest, gained all of the necessary building permits, hired contractors, and began the work in earnest. None of this would have been possible without the commitment and deep pockets of Bob Luddy. He personally signed the notes that were necessary to fund the building of a school from scratch.

The buildings were built. The staff was hired and trained. The students were lined up. The charter was in place and approved by the state. Everything was ready to go, until the State Department of Transportation got involved. The road along which we had built the school was not good enough! The State Department of Transportation would not allow us to open the school, and this was just four weeks before the school was scheduled to start classes.

Don't you just love bureaucracy? I am convinced that it was dirty politics. Some political opponent saw a way to block a charter school, or at least to cause us a tremendous headache. I was finally of some use to the board of Franklin Academy. I knew how to play politics, too. Several meetings, many phone calls, and quite a few letters later we had worked out a compromise. We lowered the speed limit on the road! We did agree to add a turning lane for those who were making a left turn into the school grounds. It was a pretty simple solution. Originally, the DOT had said that we would be required to widen the entire road, which would have cost millions and could not have been accomplished without an Environmental Impact Study which could have taken years. I sometimes take the long way around to the school so that I can use that left turn lane. It's hard for a rightwing politician to turn left, but it reminds me of how dirty politics can really get.

Today, Franklin Academy Charter School is one of the most successful charter schools in the nation. Franklin Academy is a college preparatory school that prepares its students to meet the rigorous demands of higher education. The mission statement of the school says:

> *The mission of Franklin Academy is to provide an environment that fosters and encourages high standards of academic achievement, creativity, technological sophistication, the love of learning, accountability, self esteem and the development of good citizens. In addition, it is our mission to have all students complete high school successfully, possessing the knowledge, skills, and character to become productive, responsible, and caring citizens who will meet the challenges and experience successes in their future.*

I visited the campus recently during a school day. There are several things which strike a visitor right away. The first is that the school is clean, immaculately clean. The second is that there is classical music playing through a school-wide sound system. Students learn math and English and history with classical music as a constant companion. Third, the school is quiet. It's not an oppressive quiet, but a refreshing one. Even during class changes, the students talk quietly as they walk along the halls together. No one requires this, but the students act in school much the way that most of us act in a library. To me, the quietness is a sign of respect. Fourth, the students have a dress code. The pullover knit shirts come in several colors so there is variety, but the code is strictly enforced - shirt tails tucked in, belts worn at all time. The students look neat and clean. What a radical idea that is! (When we were establishing the school, the board received more complaints from parents about the dress code than any other single item. It is now one of the things which is most appreciated by them). Fifth, there are signs of achievement everywhere! Franklin Academy celebrates achievement. Pennants on the wall of the entrance hall celebrate where each of the graduates of last year's class are attending college. On the opposite wall are pennants celebrating where teachers and staff received their degree. The halls are lined with the student's art work. This is not unusual for a school, except that the art work includes pottery, ceramics, and sculpture created in class. Did your high school have a kiln?

Franklin Academy is, quite frankly, astonishing. Its ten-year record of success is an indication that a very sound educational plan, good management, caring teachers and staff, and excellent facilities can produce outstanding students.

"Franklin Academy is a school where everyone is welcome to blossom," Bob Luddy said recently. "Most public schools are underutilizing their teachers and staff. At Franklin, we want our teachers to blossom, because we know that if they give the best of themselves to the students, the students will give the best of themselves in return," he added.

Franklin Academy has an impressive record. For the 2007 school year, the school received 1,524 applications for the 101 open spots. One of the reasons for this incredible response is that more than 90% of the students score at grade level while the state average for all public schools is about 63%.

The school does not allow fundraising except to support charities. The students will not be out selling chocolate bars in the community to support the school, but the students have requested and been given permission to support such charities as Habitat for Humanity. In addition to outstanding academics, the school has taken great pride in recent awards for music, art, technology, and engineering.

The School has been named a "School of Excellence" and it has continually surpassed state and federal standards of academic progress.

"Charter schools in general, and Franklin Academy in particular are a win-win situation since they give parents options and save taxpayer-dollars," Luddy explained in a recent article in the *News and Observer.* "We pay our teachers more than the private schools and the other public schools, so we can attract the very best. And because we are run by a local board, we can fire any teacher that is underachieving. We have been very fortunate that we have teachers with long tenures who are doing an outstanding job," he said.

While I was visiting the school recently, I was astonished by the number of computers. One student who was sitting at a computer was wearing headphones. I was a little curious about this, because in many regular public schools headphones have been banned. I asked the teacher what the student was doing, and was told that she was learning Japanese. It is one of the many self-directed electives that the school offers.

One of the goals which the board set when it applied for its charter was that students would be taught the basic character traits of honesty, self-discipline, responsibility, kindness, and respect for other students and those in authority. The school is succeeding.

That might just be a good goal for all public schools in the state.

Any time I wonder if my days of service in the legislature were worth all of the headaches and heartaches which politics can bring, I take a ride by Franklin Academy. One look restores my hope in humanity. If North Carolina just had about a thousand more Bob Luddy's out there. Maybe you are one. Give him a call. His passion will infect you.

Chapter 17

Constituent Service

"Truly, when the Day of Judgment comes, we shall not be asked what we have said, but what we have done."
—Thomas a Kempis in *Imitation of Christ*

I believe that it was Congressman Tip O'Neil, the long-time speaker of the house, who said, "All politics is local." He was right, or course. Voters do care about international and national issues like the War on Terror and NAFTA, but when an issue hits home voters really get involved. If a member of your family dies serving in the war in Afghanistan, you instantly become more interested in the course of the war. If you lose your job because the company has moved its plant to Mexico, you understand completely the effects of NAFTA.

It is in strictly local issues that voters are most likely to get involved in politics and feel its effects. Local issues are where the voters experience government on a personal level, where they can experience the good things that government does (new roads, schools, hospitals, etc.) and the bad things that government does (over regulation, unresponsiveness to the people, deteriorating infrastructure, bureaucratic red tape, etc.).

I have discovered that it is in strictly local issues that government can be the most frustrating. There are so many levels of government, so many bureaucrats who are intent on guarding their turf, so many regulations that have been passed by well-meaning legislative bodies (from town councils to congress), and so many regulations that have been put into place by bureaucrats trying to interpret or implement laws, that it can be very difficult to accomplish anything within the existing framework and nearly impossible to change the framework.

Local issues almost always have something to do with homeowners – water and sewer access, electric and gas rates, zoning, access to property (roads and bridges), noise pollution, property tax rates – this list goes on and on. Because a person's home is the largest single purchase almost every family makes in a lifetime, homeowners want to do everything in their power to guard the value of their investment. Towns and cities also know the value of houses. Property taxes are, without a doubt, the largest source of income for the counties, towns and cities. Keeping houses and neighborhoods viable and increasing in value are essential to the future of any municipality.

As a representative to the General Assembly, the majority of calls I received from voters concerned local issues. Getting involved in local politics was dangerous. It meant that I would be accused of calling into question the decisions of county boards of commissioners or town councils. As a state representative, I was often accused of sticking my nose where it didn't belong. But I believed that responding to the pleas of my constituents was a major part of my job, and if we happened to actually solve a problem along the way, so much the better.

I'd like to share a few of the local issues in which I became involved. I discovered that local politics, even more than state politics, is a lot like herding cats. It is often frustrating, but I share these stories with you so that you can see that you can, indeed, fight city hall.

The Neuse River Bridge

The bridge, which crosses the Neuse River just below the falls of the river, is a two-lane structure built in the 1940's. When Falls of Neuse Road was just a country road connecting Wake Forest and Raleigh, the bridge was adequate. But when a major new development called Wakefield was built just north of the bridge, it quickly became obsolete.

Many of the residents of Wakefield moved into their upscale homes believing that a new bridge and a widened Falls of Neuse Road were a done deal, and that a bridge had already been approved and funded.

It was when the issue of scheduling the construction came up at a meeting in 2004 that residents discovered that the done deal wasn't true. There was a preliminary plan in place for a new bridge on a new road called "New Falls of Neuse," but only the route had been set. There were no plans in place to repair, expand, or replace the existing bridge. There had also been no money allocated to build the new bridge or to replace the existing one.

The residents of Wakefield were obviously upset. The fact that the replacement bridge was not even on the drawing board meant its construction was literally years away. Adding to the problem was the shear volume of traffic, which the bridge was carrying (nearly 24,000 cars a day) and the fact that the access to the bridge (a curving, downhill two lane road on either side) was a serious safety concern.

I went to work. It was clear that the City of Raleigh had not talked with the Wake County Commissioners, that the State Department of Transportation had not been involved, and that the Capital Area Metropolitan Planning Organization (CAMPO) did not have the bridge on its agenda. The fact was that every government agency that should have taken a lead role was waiting for some other agency to act first.

My role became clear – get everybody together to actually talk. I scheduled meetings with officials of the city, county, state and even federal governments. Once people began to talk, it became very clear, very quickly, that there was a great need and that the replacement bridge and the new bridge should both be priorities.

Two great problems faced us: funding and environmental impact. Funding was something that I could actually help with. I negotiated with all of the parties involved and acquired actual dollars, not just promises. The developers of the Wakefield community contributed $500,000, the City of Raleigh $5 million and the federal government $10 million. Working directly with the office of Senator Elizabeth Dole made this possible. Another $2.5 million was to come from the State Highway Trust Fund through the Department of Transportation. With the funding in place, CAMPO put the project on its list. There were a lot a people who were greatly involved. The mayors of Raleigh and Wake Forest, Representatives of CAMPO, representatives of the DOT, and the Wake County Commissioners worked tirelessly to get the necessary approvals and funding.

The Environmental Impact Study was completely out of my control. It is astonishing to me that environmental studies take so long. One of the reasons that it will be 2009 at the very earliest before construction can begin is because of the Environment Impact Study. I am all for protecting the environment, but does it really take five years to study what effect a replacement bridge will have on the water quality?

Unfortunately, most of the time, bureaucracy can't be hurried.

Interstate 540 Noise

When Interstate 540 (the Outer Loop around Raleigh) was first planned, the state DOT took into account those existing neighborhoods which would be impacted by the constant noise of a major highway. Noise barriers were planned and built in those areas where neighborhoods existed *before* the roadway was approved.

But the DOT made it very clear that no noise barriers would be erected to shield neighborhoods which were built after the route was approved and the road constructed.

It is possible that DOT could not have anticipated the actual amount of noise. When each new section of the road was complete and opened for traffic, my office was flooded with calls from citizens who were complaining of rattling windows and a constant roar.

Part of the problem was that the finished road-bed was much higher than the original plans had called for. This meant that sound was projected into the unprotected neighborhoods. I don't know why the height of the road-bed was changed, but I suspect something to do with Environmental Impact Studies.

When I contacted the DOT about the possibility of building new sound barriers, I was met with a resounding "No!"

"Those homeowners knew when they purchased their homes that a major interstate highway was going to be right next door. The DOT can't be responsible for someone buying a home that they later regretted buying," was the general response that I received.

But there had to be some kind of compromise. If sound walls couldn't be built, was there some other way of diffusing the sound? Again, it was a matter of getting people to sit down and talk. There really was an effective compromise.

Instead of erecting a brick or concrete wall, numerous trees would be planted. Not only would the trees grow to become an effective sound barrier, but they would add beauty to the roadway and provide effective erosion control. The compromise was reached, the trees were planted, and 540 is now one of the most beautiful urban interstates in the nation.

Sometimes government actually gets it right.

Zebulon Flood

When Hurricane Floyd devastated North Carolina, most of my district was spared major damage. But there was one small neighborhood in Zebulon that was badly flooded. I received a phone call from one of the residents of a subdivision called Pineview Estates. I got in the car and drove to Zebulon. When I got to the neighborhood, I was surprised by the devastation.

Running along the edge of the subdivision was a sewer line. The manhole entrances for the line were all elevated on mounds about six feet high. When I saw these mounds, I asked the resident who called me if the water had risen above the manhole covers.

"No," she said. "The water never got that high."

Those elevated manhole covers told me all I needed to know. The engineers who designed the sewer system knew that the neighborhood was in a flood plain, which meant that the town of Zebulon knew.

In fact, the Federal Emergency Management Association (FEMA) maps clearly showed that the neighborhood was in a flood plain. So FEMA knew. The builder knew. The town knew. But none of the homeowners knew.

As a result, none of the homeowners had flood insurance. Mortgage companies require flood insurance when homes are built in a flood plain. But the mortgage companies had been kept in the dark as well.

My role, once again, was to get people together to talk. When the meetings were held, there was a lot of finger pointing. The builder, the town officials, the state and federal representatives all knew the danger and knew that permits to build in the area should not have been issued.

There were a lot of angry people at the meetings. The homeowners were angry. The mortgage companies were angry. The town officials were angry (they had gotten caught issuing building permits that should never have been issued). FEMA officials were angry because their maps had been ignored (except for the sewer system).

Of all of the people who were angry, the town officials were the most upset...with me! They were angry that I had gotten involved at all. The issue was too local for me to have anything to do with it. My presence was ruffling some very sensitive feathers.

It seemed to me that although there was plenty of blame to spread around, the town officials were the most at fault. I was stunned that there is no provision in state law to require towns and cities to inform residents that they are living in a flood plain.

"If they are taking tax money from these people," I said in an interview at the time, "then they should be required to notify them. This is common courtesy. You shouldn't have to have a law to do something that is common decency for the citizens of your town."

I threatened to introduce a bill requiring municipalities and real estate agents to disclose that homes were built in a flood plain. The threat was all that was needed. The towns and cities in my district agreed that notification would be their policy in the future.

It didn't help the homeowners in Pineview Estates very much. They would spend months in litigation and in negotiation with insurance and mortgage companies. But hopefully, it improved the chances of future homeowners to know the truth about their property.

Wake Forest Water

Water is one of the most important commodities any town or city controls. The amount of water available to a city directly determines its growth. The town of Wake Forest has seen unprecedented growth in the last decade. The town has managed the growth by purchasing water from the City of Raleigh to augment its modest supply.

Raleigh has also had tremendous growth, and, looking to the future, wanted to set growth limits on water usage from the municipalities which were buying water from them.

On Highway 1, halfway between Raleigh and Wake Forest, there is an abandoned Burlington Industries cloth manufacturing plant. When the plant was in operation, 5,000,000 gallons of water a day would be drawn from the Neuse to use in the company's dyeing operations, filtered, and then discharged back into the Neuse.

Wake Forest officials saw this "intake" as a solution to their growth problem. They proposed to tap into the old intake and pump the maximum amount of water allowed into the city's system. The city of Raleigh objected, strenuously.

If Wake Forest was permitted to pump 5,000,000 gallons of water day from the Neuse, the City of Raleigh would have to release an equal amount from its Falls Lake Reservoir to maintain the proper flow of the Neuse. Cities all along the Neuse have entered into a pact to keep the flow of the river at a constant level.

I became involved when many citizens of Wake Forest contacted me to express their concern. For many citizens, the numbers just didn't add up. The town of Wake Forest was proposing pumping water from the Neuse, building a water treatment plant, and laying the pipes and pumping system to distribute the water to its residents. The result was going to be much higher water bills for all of the citizens of Wake Forest.

In this case there was already a lot of talk going on. The two municipalities had been holding meetings for nearly a year when I got involved. Charges were being tossed about and the press had become very involved. When I showed up at one of the public hearings on the matter, neither the Wake Forest nor Raleigh officials were glad to see me.

"What are you doing here?" one of them pointedly asked me. "This is a strictly local matter," he added.

"I'm just here as a concerned citizen," I said. "I'm just here to listen and to learn." Apparently state legislators don't just attend public hearings as concerned citizens. My presence was a threat.

I have never gotten involved in a problem where the feelings ran higher. And the more involved I became the greater threat I seemed to be. I even had one lobbyist come to my office in the legislative building and literally intimidate me. His words were as close to an actual threat of violence as any I heard in my twelve years in the assembly.

I used my office in the legislative building to get the various parties together. The folks from Wake Forest didn't want to meet in the Raleigh City Hall and the Raleigh folks thought that it was beneath their dignity to go to Wake Forest. My office was neutral territory. Despite all of the meetings, no progress was being made. The town of Wake Forest had entered into a binding agreement with all of the other municipalities along the Neuse about the amount of water that they could draw each day. To begin using the Burlington Industries intake would break that agreement which would have opened up a flood of problems for all of the towns and cities along the Neuse.

Eventually, I introduced a bill that gave the parties six months to work out a deal to merge the Wake Forest and Raleigh systems. The deadline was January 1, 2005. If a deal was not struck, Wake Forest would be required to fully comply with its earlier agreement which meant that it would have no opportunity for growth.

At the very last minute, December 30th, a compromise was reached. The Raleigh and Wake Forest water systems were merged; Raleigh agreed to increase capacity to Wake Forest so that the town could have steady growth; and the merger did not raise the water rates of the citizens of Wake Forest.

I have often wondered if the whole exercise was simply the town of Wake Forest pushing hard for the best deal it could get from Raleigh or if the town had no real intention of using the Burlington intake. I don't know. All I do know is that after a year's worth of meetings, the compromise was a win-win situation. To butcher a quote about the gods, "The mills of politics grind slowly, but they grind exceedingly well."

Chapter 18

Family Feud

"All political parties die, in the end, of swallowing their own lies."
—RALPH WALDO EMERSON

There is an ongoing debate within the North Carolina Republican Party that affects the very soul of the party and how it operates in the state. The debate centers on the central question "What is the role of government?" The party is divided into two distinctive camps: Progressive Republicans and Conservative Republicans.

Essentially, Progressive Republicans see the need for government. Progressives realize that there are some things, which the government should do and that it is necessary for Republicans and Democrats to work together to accomplish those things (like providing education, roads, healthcare, prisons).

Conservative Republicans are distrustful of government. Though Conservatives also see the need for some government, their main goal is to limit government as much as possible. Conservative Republicans are proud guardians of what have been called traditional values, and are working hard to thwart any movement towards liberalization of these values. Conservative Republicans are convinced that any compromise with the Democrats, on any issue, is a pact with the Devil.

The great debate really focuses on whether or not a representative in the General Assembly can be both Progressive and Conservative at the same time. Unlike some other states, there are no "liberal" Republicans serving in the North Carolina Legislature. All of the Republican representatives are conservative, but even the Conservatives are divided. There are philosophical differences between those who believe that fiscal conservatism (cutting taxes and spending) should be the central thrust of the party's agenda as opposed to social conservatism (abortion, gay marriage, death penalty, etc) carrying the day.

Most Republicans have a strong independent streak. This is both a blessing and a curse. It is a blessing because Republicans tend to stand strongly for what they believe, and it is a curse because it keeps Republicans from forming an effective governing coalition. During my time in the House, I was amazed that the Republican Caucus could never come to a consensus. While the Republican Caucus was meeting, the Democratic Caucus would also be holding their session. Though they were behind closed doors, we could hear the Democrats fighting and fussing among themselves. But no matter how much they fought among themselves, when they emerged from their caucus meetings, the Democrats would be united. With a strong, united front, the Democrats could effectively run the legislature.

As I served in the assembly, it became apparent to me that part of the problem, which Republicans faced, was that much of our agenda was not coming to us from the grassroots. The Republican agenda was so fractured that there was no way to form a true governing consensus. There was a need to have much stronger input and direction from the rank and file Republicans in the state. The grassroots Republicans were being ignored because the power brokers (those who gave the big bucks to the party and individual candidates) were dominating the decision making process.

This lack of involvement by the little people led me to seek the Chairmanship of the North Carolina Republican Party in 1997. I ran a campaign based on the idea that the state convention could, and should, draw thousands of Republicans instead of hundreds. It was my firm belief, and I still hold to it, that the convention could be the catalyst for dramatic change within the party and the state.

The Republican Convention has been an expensive, exclusive gathering. In fact, the convention has become nothing more than an elaborate fundraising event. The vast majority of local Republicans has never attended the convention, has no input into the agenda of the convention, and, in fact, has never been invited to attend. The party has not used all of the technology available to garner grassroots participation. And there has been a distinct lack of support for Republican candidates who are seeking local and state offices.

Even though I ran a spirited campaign for chairman, the sitting chairman did as well. He argued that the powerbrokers were the ones funding the organization, that the party was making great strides in the state, and that a "if it's not broke, don't fix it policy" should prevail. His points of view eventually won the day, and he was reelected.

But the issues that I raised are still with the party, and have, in effect, become more prominent since 1997. *The News and Observer* columnist Rob Christiansen has described the infighting in the Republican Party as a "civil war." I agree with him.

The war became especially evident in 2002 when the Republicans won a slim 61-59 majority in the House. We lost that majority when a Republican switched parties and became a Democrat. The equally divided House was deadlocked. It was clear that nothing was going to be accomplished. There were many Republicans who thought that a do nothing House was a great idea. These Republicans were especially angry with the fact that this desertion had cost them their positions of power. Other Republicans felt that some kind of compromise with the Democrats was essential and that the purpose of the House was to actually govern the state – to do something. A Republican representative led a five-member GOP faction that forged a coalition with Democratic House leaders. A Republican and a Democrat served as co-speakers, but one of the negative effects of the deal was that many Republicans found themselves out of power – important committee chairmanships were lost.

I was not one of the five Republicans who formed the coalition. I have been linked to them because once it became obvious that the coalition was going to win and that the power sharing was going to take effect, I joined many other Republicans in the House to support the compromise. The feud among House Republicans was made worse by powerful Republicans who were not in the House but whose influence and money were used to defeat Republicans who formed the coalition in the 2004 election.

The Republican Legislative Majority of North Carolina is what is known as a 527 committee. A 527 is a committee that is a direct result of the McCain-Feingold Legislation in the U.S. Congress. A 527 is an organization whose purpose is to "inform" voters and to be an "advocacy group" for a certain issue. It is against the law for a 527 to directly influence an election. The Republican Legislative Majority of North Carolina was founded and supported by just one Republican whose purpose was to defeat those Republicans who had compromised.

It turned out to be politics at its dirtiest! In the 2006 election, I became one of the main targets of the 527. I was linked to Jim Black. In fact, one of the postcards, which was sent to many households in my District showed me "chained" to Democratic Speaker Jim Black. I had made the unpardonable sin of wanting the House to actually govern. I lost my primary election.

The infighting which began long before the compromise only got worse after it. The House Republicans fought over redistricting, taxes, budgets and all kinds of social issues. I remember one especially divisive issue which was proposed simply to put Republicans in an impossible position politically. A law was proposed that would make it legal for a mother to abandon her baby if she left it at an active fire station. It was a political nightmare. If you voted for the bill, you could be accused of voting to abandon babies. If you voted against the bill, you could be accused of hating single moms who had no other recourse. Strangely enough, the bill was introduced by Republicans to embarrass other Republicans.

It is clear that Republicans in North Carolina have not heeded the advice of President Ronald Reagan when he said, "Never speak evil of another Republican."

Because it was clear to other members of the Republican delegation that I really believed that a legislator could be conservative and progressive at the same time, I was given leadership roles within the House that I did not seek. One of the most difficult of these was to be the Republican chair of the redistricting effort. Every ten years, after the U.S. Census, the U.S. House Districts and the N.C. Senate and House Districts must be redrawn to reflect (in the case of the U.S. House) the growth of population, and in the case of the General Assembly both the growth and shifting of the population. [The State of North Carolina is growing rapidly, but the northeastern counties are losing population.] Redistricting makes everybody mad. The state is required by the federal courts to have a number of minority majority districts (the number changes after each census). These minority majority districts are a good thing in that they assure that all voices will be represented in the legislature, but they are a bad thing in that they give the Democrats a built-in advantage. Republicans were also at a disadvantage because we were not negotiating from a position of strength. The Democrats knew that we were fighting among ourselves. We were so weakened, that we were lucky to even be at the table. Democrats were gerrymandering. So was I.

District lines are so important that they actually come down to every single address. Technology should make the process easier. With computer maps of all of the households in North Carolina, including breakdowns by race, voter registration, economic diversity, it should be almost a no brainer. But, believe me, it's tough. As the process progressed, and members of the legislature would see the proposed changes in their districts, I was assailed! I remember telling the House Republican leader, who had appointed me, "This redistricting may very well cost me my seat, but I will do what I can for the benefit of the state." When the final map was presented, it was, at first, well received. Two very conservative groups in the state, NCFree and The John Locke Foundation, both initially proclaimed the new districts a win for Republicanism. But after a few disgruntled House Republicans complained about their new districts, the statewide Republican Party announced their opposition and accused me of "giving away the house." It is interesting to me that the Republicans did not blame the Democrats who controlled the votes and the process.

The infighting continues. The result is that Republicans have not won a majority in the NC Senate since the 1870's and have controlled the House for only four years in that same period of time. Republicans have a problem recruiting good candidates – why would anyone want to step into the middle of a feud? – and the party doesn't support the candidates that we do have.

I have often wondered why I was willing to take on the extra, no-win duties. Maybe it goes back to my childhood and my dad's insistence that we always have something more to do. Maybe it is the challenge. Maybe it is because I like to try and be a part of the solution to problems.

I believe that the Republican Party in North Carolina must figure out a way to do something productive and to make positive changes. I understand the need for the party to be obstructionists sometimes. I have added my vote many times to stop some piece of legislation, and I am proud of it. But I also believe that we cannot just be the party which stops things.

If the Republicans are ever going to have a majority in the General Assembly, we must learn to listen, really listen, to the people of North Carolina. That means we need to listen to our opponents. Many members of the GOP have the notion that listening is selling your soul. But I completely disagree. If we listen, really listen, we will develop a true grassroots strategy, which will sweep us into power. And if we listen, really listen, we will govern effectively.

Republicans need to learn to disagree agreeably. Until we do, we will always have a fractured soul.

Chapter 19

What I Learned from Politics

"Democracy is the worst form of government in the world, except for all the others."
—WINSTON CHURCHILL

I had only been in the General Assembly for a few months when I was asked to represent the House at the planting of the "Peace Rose" at the governor's mansion. The Peace Rose is a symbol of Victim's Rights and was to be planted at the mansion to be a perpetual reminder to the governor of his responsibility to care for the victims of crime. It was also to serve as a reminder to the families of crime victims that the government really does care about things like justice and fairness.

The morning of the ceremony the sky was grey and threatening rain. Just as I arrived at the governor's mansion, a steady rain began to fall, and the decision was made to move the "planting" inside. Seats were hastily set up in the parlor of the mansion for the dignitaries who were present. I had never been in the governor's mansion. (The only time I had come close was when I toured the mansion grounds as a seventh grader, the year in school that all students in North Carolina were required to study state history).

I hung back in the crowd. There were a lot of folks there – representatives of the North Carolina Victims Assistance Network, the judiciary, the legislature, the justice department, the North Carolina Council of Churches, and many more. I was enjoying just looking around as I waited for the ceremony to begin, when, much to my surprise; I was escorted to a seat directly beside the governor!

Me and the Governor

From Mammy's outhouse to a seat in the governor's mansion was quite a giant step for a country boy from Rolesville. It was one thing to be one of 120 members of the House. Walking into the legislative building on Jones Street for the first time had been incredible and awe inspiring. But this was almost overwhelming. Who was I to be sitting next to the governor?

He was actually talking to me, just like I was a real person. I don't remember much about the ceremony, but I do remember that early on in the proceedings someone was called upon to lead a prayer.

Not only was I sitting next to the governor, I was praying with him! During the prayer, I kept hearing clicking noises that sounded an awful lot like cameras.

"Why would photographers be taking pictures during a prayer?" I asked myself. I must admit that I decided to take a peek, and I was surprised that all of the press photographers had gathered right in front of the governor and me to take pictures of the governor and a legislator praying. I suppose that it is an astonishing thing, in the days of separation of church and state, to have a picture of the governor and a state legislator praying together. It was a picture that would run in almost every newspaper in the state. I was just glad that none of the photographs showed me peeking.

It was one of those wonderful moments that politics can provide. A Democratic governor and a Republican legislator sitting side-by-side, joining together to celebrate the fact some things are more important than party and partisan bickering. As I prayed with the governor, and as the ceremony continued, I realized that sometimes the government actually gets it right, that sometimes politics is a good thing, and that sometimes political bickering and infighting can be set aside and statesmanship can rule the day.

Believe it or not, there really are some good things about politics. Being involved in politics is one of the best educations that any person can receive. I'd like to share with you some of the lessons I learned, some of the valuable truths about how to be a successful politician. They are lessons which are applicable to all walks of life.

Care About Others

One of the great traps of politics is that it is easy to be overcome by the power of the office. Just after I was elected to the legislature, I received an official letter from the state addressed to The Honorable Rick Eddins. Wow.

"I must be important," I thought. Winning an election had given me instant credibility. I was now an "honorable" man.

Unfortunately, not all politicians stay honorable. I am sure that almost every politician begins his or her term in office with grand hopes. Most have grand plans as well. But politicians quickly get hit in the face with politics.

Change doesn't happen nearly as fast it should – certainly not as fast as I would have liked it to. Politics is down right frustrating. It is almost impossible to change an existing law, and creating a new law, though a little bit easier, requires the patience of Job.

One of the reasons that politics can be so frustrating is that politicians often forget why they ran for office in the first place. Most politicians really do care about other people and want to do what is best. But politics often gets in the way of caring, power often trumps compassion, and party loyalty can corrupt. If politicians would take an oath to remember that caring about others is the essence of government, politics would always be the noble endeavor it was intended to be.

Learn to Listen

There are three sides to every political argument: the right side, the wrong side, and the middle. The middle is where almost every politician finds himself on every issue. There are good people on all sides; good people with differing views. The government never has complete consensus. There are always people who disagree with every decision that is made.

I was a politician who believed that it was important to listen to all sides. I believed that listening, really listening, gave me openness to new ideas. Listening brought me a great deal of respect and a great deal of criticism. The critics said that just listening to opposing views made me a compromiser and that I was guilty of surrendering my conservative credentials.

But for most people, my willingness to listen garnered their respect. Most of the time people just want to be heard. They understand that not everyone will agree with them, but if you take the time to listen, really listen, you may find that you are closer together on an issue than you thought possible. That is not always true, of course. Some people are just off the wall, but even those who are diametrically opposed to your point of view have a right to be heard.

Since politicians are almost always stuck in the middle, it is essential that they listen to the voices that come from either side. It is from the middle that almost all legislation is born. Politicians who listen to only one point of view end up offering legislation that has no chance of becoming law.

Be Tactful

My former Pastor, Dr. Bob O'Keef, defined tact in one of his sermons as "the ability to tell a man to go to hell and have him look forward to the trip." I don't know that I have that much tact, but I have learned that tact is essential if a politician wants to be part of the solution and not just part of the problem. Tact is the unique ability to speak the truth without giving too much offense. It is impossible to accomplish anything in politics if you are constantly offending those who are on the opposite side of the aisle or those in your own party with whom you have differences. Genuine differences of opinion exist, and always will.

There are some politicians that I would love to have told to "go to hell." Many of them were fellow Republicans. I am sure that there were many who felt the same way about me. But because of this wonderful thing called tact, civility existed in the halls of the General Assembly.

It is a shame that politicians don't use the same civility outside of the legislative building that they do inside. It is in the election cycles that politics truly loses civility. In opinion polls, the public always says that it hates dirty politics and negative advertising, but the fact is that those things tend to work. Negative ads have been with us since before the founding of our country and always will be. The longer a politician is in office the more opportunity there is for his opponents to wage a negative campaign. Every vote in the legislature is a possible political land mine. And politics is rampant with opponents waging war against each other by skewing each other's record.

Sometimes, it is impossible to speak the truth tactfully. Jesus looked the Pharisees in the eye and said to them, "You are just white washed tombs, pretty and washed on the outside, but full of death on the inside." I don't think the Pharisees appreciated this truth very much. They decided that the only way to deal with Jesus was to kill him. I'm glad that my political opponents decided to attack just my record and not my life.

Give Others Credit

In each session of the General Assembly, there are between 3,000 and 4,000 new bills introduced. There is no way that there are 4,000 good ideas every session. Usually the assembly ends up passing into law about one tenth of the bills that are introduced.

It takes a majority of both houses of the assembly to pass a bill. Legislators who have a good idea should be given ownership of that idea. Unfortunately, that is not always the case. Because Democrats control the legislature, they are unwilling to give credit to any Republican. And because Republicans are in the minority, they are reluctant to admit that Democrats can have a good idea.

This is one of the truly petty problems which the legislature must face. Politicians from both parties need to learn to give credit to others, or at least be willing to. When a politician of either party comes up with one of the thirty or forty really good ideas (out of 4,000) that come before the assembly each session, it should be something that everyone celebrates. If a really good idea becomes a really good law, all of the politicians in the state should honor that person's creativity and take credit for supporting the idea.

If a member of the minority party has a really good idea but can't get it heard because he is in the minority, he needs to learn the power of giving up ownership of his bill so that it can become law. If it is a really good idea, a member of the majority will be glad to sponsor the legislation and take credit for it. It is just a shame that politics is often so petty!

Be Honest and Consistent

Every person who is elected to the General Assembly has instant credibility. The fact that he or she has won an election and is sworn into the office gives them a place of honor and responsibility within the state government. Each legislator can keep his credibility or lose it. Each legislator can build relationships of trust with the other legislators.

The running of the General Assembly is based on mutual trust. If you are a member of the assembly and you tell another member that you will do something, and then do the opposite, you will have lost that member's trust. And he or she will tell all of the other members, "You can't trust..." Having once lost your credibility, it can never be regained. Politicians understand that there will be differences of opinion. They don't expect members of the other party to agree with them, and they understand that sometimes even members of their own party will disagree. But when a member promises to support another member and then does the opposite, his effectiveness in the assembly is destroyed.

Be Loyal to Your Friends

In politics, it is essential to have friends. Since it is impossible to accomplish anything in the legislature as a lone wolf, building bonds of trust and friendship with other members is essential.

There are obviously different levels of friendship. You can't be bosom buddies with every other member of the assembly, or city council, or county board of commissioners. But if you are not loyal to your true friends, you obviously can't expect them to be loyal to you.

Sometimes a friend will have a piece of legislation that you are not wild about. It's not going to do any particular harm, but you don't see it doing much good either. As long as it isn't a bad idea, loyalty necessitates supporting your friend. The time will come when one of your not bad ideas will need his or her support.

There are a lot of good things about politics. It is nice to accomplish something good. It is a wonderful thing to serve the needs of the people who elected you. It is a heartwarming and gratifying experience to make a lasting change in the political landscape of the state. It is equally gratifying to keep some things from happening. One of the most frequent things that voters said to me (and I guess to most members of the House) was "Don't do anything. Keep the government out of our lives!"

Whether we like it or not, government and politics are involved in every aspect of our lives. From the water we drink and use for our sewers to the food which we buy, government is involved. From the electricity we use in our homes to the gas we burn in our cars, politics plays a part. Politics is involved, in one way or another, in the manufacture, distribution, and sale of every consumer product. So it is essential that politicians care about the people that they represent, and seek to limit the government's control while providing for the public's safety.

Our system of government was created to move slowly. As I said elsewhere in this book, gridlock is a good thing. The founding fathers of America knew that government which moves too quickly makes too many mistakes. Even though the plodding, snail's pace of legislative government is frustrating, it is far less frustrating than a government which moves without thought and deliberation.

When George Washington, late in his political career, was asked "What is the secret to good government in a democracy?" he answered, "Compromise, compromise, compromise. But never compromise your principles." Politicians have always had to deal with the influence that big money can bring to the debate. Big money, and the lobbyists which it funds, are both a constant enemy and constant friend of the General Assembly. Big money is constantly seeking to influence the legislators to do something. Sometimes the something that the powerbrokers want done is a good thing, and sometimes it is something which would require a member to compromise his or her principles. That is why money is both an enemy and a friend of politics.

Politics is a good thing as long as you can compromise enough to get some things done, but not so much that you lose your integrity.

Representative Rick Eddins

When I was voted out of the legislature, I wondered if I had compromised too much, or not enough. I certainly felt that I had somehow lost the public's trust. Certainly, the skewed opposition that I received during the campaign from within my own party contributed to the public's perception of me. I was portrayed as someone who had compromised too much, as a Republican who was in the pocket of the Democrats.

All I know for sure is that when I cleaned out my office at the legislature and turned in my keys to the building, I had a deep sense of loss. I believe that I had served the best interests of the state and my district. I held my head high as I walked from the building. My heart may have been broken, but my convictions weren't.

Chapter 20

Where Do We Go from Here?

"We have it in our power to begin the world over again."
—THOMAS PAINE IN *COMMON SENSE*

This book has not been a platform for me to seek another term in the House or to seek any other elected office. However, I hope that it may have motivated some of the readers to get involved in business or politics, or to volunteer in some way to make a positive difference in our state.

There are still so many issues which the government must face. The government will never solve all of the problems which face us. Each time the state rises to meet some crisis, another one will rise to take its place. But there are some critical issues which must be addressed.

Education

Every failing school is a breeding ground for Central Prison. The vast majority of the inmates in our prison system are adults that never received a proper education. Some of the prisoners failed because they made poor choices. Some failed because the schools they attended failed them.

Every failing school is also a breeding ground for the underemployed. Students who graduate without an ability to read are not much use to any employer. Students who can't do simple math can't even be cashiers down at the country store.

If even one child falls through the cracks and doesn't receive the education that he or she should have received, that is a failure which the entire population of the state must bear.

You have already read two chapters about charter schools, so you know that I strongly support the expansion of the charter school movement within the state. The state needs to think outside of the box and try some new things. The School of Science and Mathematics in Durham and the North Carolina School of the Arts in Winston-Salem are perfect examples of doing things out of the box. Both of the schools have been tremendously successful. Shouldn't the state figure out ways to expand the concept? If something is working, shouldn't the state duplicate it over and over again?

The legislature is not listening to the outcry of protest from parents of our public school children. Maybe the NCEA makes more noise than the parents; they certainly give more money to the politicians. The legislature is in a bit of a conundrum – local school boards want state money but they don't like state (or federal) mandates. It is clear that the state must mandate reform.

The state should try ten pilot projects where parents who must send their students to a failing inner city school would be given a tax credit to send those same children to a private school. Study the students for two years and see if it has made a difference. Charter schools need to be expanded from a maximum of 100 statewide to as many as the public will support.

These kinds of bold initiatives to strengthen public education in the state will not happen until more parents become radically involved. The outcry of the parents needs to be so loud and so pervasive that the government simply must listen.

State Budgeting

The last state budget, which I considered as a member of the House in 2005, was $33,810,611,674. Most taxpayers have never heard the total amount. They may have heard that the general fund budget was just over $17 billion, but that is just roughly half of what the state spends each year.

State spending is out of control. The budget, as it is presented to the legislators, has too many "R's" (recurring) and not enough "NR's" (nonrecurring). Like most state and federal governments, the vast majority of our spending is on recurring programs. The duplications in programs are unbelievable. I don't remember the exact figures, but I seem to remember that there are 37 different job training programs which the state funds and all of which have a big R beside their cost in the budget. Every single one of the programs is doing the exact same thing, but no one in the legislature has the power (if you're in the minority) or the courage (if you're in the majority) to demand a streamlining of the government.

The state budget must become a zero based budget. The state needs to start over and justify every cent that is spent. There are only two ways that this might happen. The first way is for a really strong governor to take the bull by the horns and use his or her power in the executive branch to require that each department cut out duplication and overspending. (Some experts say that the budget could be cut by up to 20% without effecting true government services. I don't know if that is true or not, but it sounds about right to me).

The second way for the state to get control of its spending would be to elect some other party than the Democrats into the majority of the General Assembly. Since the Democrats have controlled the assembly for over 140 years, it seems that the public is okay with overspending. I'm not holding my breath for this option.

I suppose that a third possible solution would be a taxpayer revolt of some kind. I used to say that I didn't mind paying my state taxes because I saw the money doing some good (like roads, bridges, and schools), but now I'm not so sure if the state isn't following the pattern of the federal government. Wasteful spending is theft. The government is stealing from the taxpayers.

Highway Construction

The citizens of the state of North Carolina pay the highest gasoline taxes in the South. We pay this high tax to fund the Highway Trust Fund. The fund is also supported by a highway use tax, paid mostly by truckers, and title fees. In 2005, the state received 1.93 billion dollars for the Highway Trust Fund.

What most citizens don't know is that the legislature has mandated by law that *at least $173 million* of the trust fund money be transferred to the general fund each year. In 2005, the General Assembly voted to transfer nearly $253 million in spite of the fact that we had a budget *surplus.*

Road construction is one of the most important functions of the state. Though we have a wonderful network of roads, there are literally billions of dollars of road projccts which must be addressed. The northeastern and western counties of the state have been especially neglected when it comes to new, or even improved, roads.

One of the major sources of road construction money is the federal government, but federal money carries with it federal mandates. The most difficult mandates to comply with are the Environmental Impact Studies. It takes years for the studies to be completed, but new roads are seldom denied. Nobody wants to harm the environment, but good roads are essential to a strong economy and a strong economy is essential to a state that wants to continue to increase its general fund spending.

Two solutions have been suggested to help solve the problem of unbuilt and unimproved roads. The first is a tax increase. Recently, a member of the House recommended that the gasoline tax be increased by another 10 cents a gallon. The second option is to add toll roads. The first toll road in the state will be opened as a part of Interstate 540 (though the part with tolls on it will be called NC 540 because no one bothered to get federal approval for the toll). One of the major construction projects which the state faces in the not too distant future is the rebuilding and widening of I-95, one of the most heavily traveled roads in our state. A $10 toll has been proposed.

I am opposed both to a tax increase and tolls. We simply need to stop stealing from the Highway Trust Fund. In addition to the trust fund, the voters have approved billions in bonds for road and bridge construction. We need to put highways on the fast track. There is no reason for it to take 20 years to build a road or a bridge.

Taxes

If the spending crisis in the state were solved, we could cut taxes across the board and improve our infrastructure at the same time. I don't know why anybody would be opposed to that.

But many legislators are. Every year the General Assembly raises taxes in one form or another. The time has come for a taxpayer protection act – a law, which would tie spending to population growth and inflation. This act has been proposed by Republican legislators each session of the legislature for years. Democrats have never allowed it to even come before a committee for a hearing.

Social Issues

As they say in the church, I know that I am about to go from preaching to meddling, but it is important that someone stand up for traditional virtues. I use the word, virtues, on purpose. Everyone throws around the word values these days, but it doesn't mean anything. Everybody has values, but not everyone practices virtues.

The state needs to return to some old fashioned virtues: truth and honesty in public service, patriotism, celebrating hard work and success, and faith. And the state needs to recognize that the vast majority of the voters live by those virtues. In support of these virtues and many others, the state needs to pass Jessica's Law, to strengthen the Son of Sam Law, to limit parole eligibility for hardened criminals, to ban gay marriage (even if a constitutional amendment is needed), to fund adoption agencies and adoption services, to fight funding of abortion, and to find some way to stop activist judges who are legislating from the bench.

I know that the stands that I have taken on these issues mark me as a "right winger," especially in the eyes of Liberals. I am proud to wear the label.

Remember, earlier in the book, I said that God was watching while I served in the General Assembly. He still is.

Chapter 21

Floating Along

"Those who think themselves too smart to engage in politics are punished by being governed by those who are dumber."

—PLATO

During the terms that I served in the House under co-speakers, I was asked to fulfill one of the most important roles in politics – to be the floater. Floaters are members of the House who are given the vote in every committee. For some reason, in the power-sharing agreement between the Democrats and the Republicans, the Democrats had three floaters and the Republicans only two.

Floaters are a perfect example of everything that is good about politics and everything that is bad about politics. Floaters are good for politics because they are persons who have to have their finger on the pulse of every piece of legislation. Floaters have to be aware of the intricate ins and outs of the assembly; to be aware of the ever-changing schedule, to know what is coming up for vote and how close the vote might be. The assembly is all about counting votes. The process of vote counting is continual, and has very little to do with the actual vote on any piece of legislation. The outcome of most bills is decided long before any vote is taken. Floaters are important on controversial issues because they can help determine the outcome of a bill by voting in the committee. In a closely divided House, the floater was often the person whose vote decided the fate of a bill.

Floaters are bad because they show the pure pettiness of politics. Most of my votes as the floater were determined by the party caucus, and the vast majority was for the purpose of stopping the Democrats. The Democratic floaters were doing the same thing, of course, to the Republicans. To be honest, there were times that I was grateful that I had the power to stop some things, but there were many other times that my vote seemed incredibly petty. America's founding fathers dreamed of politicians being able to rise above politics, but that dream has become a nightmare.

In spite of the bad side of the role, I enjoyed being the floater. Keeping myself abreast of all of the issues that came before the House made me more and more aware of the intricacies of government, of the good that government can do, and of the unbelievable harm that government can do.

It is a great irony to me that I now find myself floating, not quite sure where life is leading me. Being out of office has some good points: the phone isn't ringing off the hook every night; my family isn't being stressed with the dirtiness of politics; I do not have to deal with negative campaigns and the ongoing distortion of my record. But I also miss the good side of politics: being able to give personal help to someone in my district; being involved in the great social debates of our times; bringing positive change to the state; and helping to make the government more responsive to the needs of the people.

It is my hope that in sharing my journey through life, through business, and through politics, that others will come to realize that individuals can, indeed, make a difference; that life is worth living to its fullest; that God will use us for good if we listen to His call and obey His direction; and that, working with others, we can win the great political, cultural, and economic contests which we face!

I invite you to join the battle.

www.ingramcontent.com/pod-product-compliance
Lightning Source LLC
LaVergne TN
LVHW090955080826
845145LV00003B/1018

* 9 7 8 1 5 9 9 3 2 0 8 8 5 *